Jenny Thomas and Diane White

NELSON
CENGAGE Learning

Australia • Brazil • Japan • Korea • Mexico • Singapore • Spain • United Kingdom • United States

**Achievement English @ Year 13**
**2nd Edition**
**Jenny Thomas**
**Diane White**

Cover designer: Book Design Ltd www.bookdesign.co.nz
Text designer: Book Design Ltd www.bookdesign.co.nz
Production controller: Siew Han Ong

Any URLs contained in this publication were checked for currency during the production process. Note, however, that the publisher cannot vouch for the ongoing currency of URLs.

First published in 2005 by New House

**Acknowledgements**

Our grateful thanks to all past and present colleagues who have so generously shared their expertise, creativity and resources. English departments thrive on your collegiality.

The authors and publisher wish to thank the following people and organisations for permission to use the resources in this textbook. Every effort has been made to trace and acknowledge all copyright owners of material used in this book. In most cases this was successful and copyright is acknowledged as requested. However, if any infringement has occurred the publishers tender their apologies and invite the copyright holders to contact them.

Page 8, Auckland University Press for Under the Pines by Rhian Gallagher; page 26, Longacre Press for *Fire and Ice* by Tania Roxborogh; page 23, Colin Rowbotham for *Dissection*; page 31, Penguin Books (UK) and *The Power and the Glory* by Graham Greene; page 32, ALIVE and Southern Cross for *Our Evolving Language* by Max Cryer; page 35, David Hill for *Zero Tolerance on Holiday roads? What a good idea*; page 38, Frank Sargeson Trust and Random House for *Memoirs of a Peon* by Frank Sargeson; page 40, The Estate of Eric Blair for *Down and Out in Paris and London* by George Orwell; page 42, Auckland University Press for *Along Rideout Road That Summer* by Maurice Duggan; page 48, Penguin Books (UK) for *Cider with Rosie* by Laurie Lee; page 52, New Zealand Herald for *Peter Lyons reckons he has what it takes ...* by Peter Lyons; page 54, The Sydney Morning Herald for *Light of my life: with buttons and glows, you're not just a pretty fascia* by Danny Katz; page 63, Enitharmon Press for *A Case of Murder* by Vernon Scannell; page 66, Faber and Faber (UK) for *An Arundel Tomb* by Philip Larkin; page 70, Faber and Faber (UK) for *Metaphors* by Sylvia Plath; page 74, Farrar, Straus and Giroux for *Death of a Naturalist* by Seamus Heaney; page 76, Elizabeth Smither for *My parents dancing*; page 78, Random House for *You're Telling Me* by Emma Neale, page 89, Henry Holt and Company for *Fire and Ice* by Robert Frost; page 94, The Independent (UK) for *Residence Fit for a King of kings* by Cahal Milmo.



For product information and technology assistance,
in Australia call **1300 790 853**;
in New Zealand call **0800 449 725**

For permission to use material from this text or product, please email **aust.permissions@cengage.com**

**National Library of New Zealand Cataloguing-in-Publication Data**
Thomas, Jenny, 1972-
Achievement English @ year 13 / Jenny Thomas and Diane White. 2nd ed.
Previous ed.: 2005.
ISBN 978-017023-329-3
1. English language—Rhetoric.
I. White, Diane. II. Title.
808.042—dc 23

**Cengage Learning Australia**
Level 7, 80 Dorcas Street
South Melbourne, Victoria Australia 3205

**Cengage Learning New Zealand**
Unit 4B Rosedale Office Park
331 Rosedale Road, Albany, North Shore 0632, NZ

For learning solutions, visit **cengage.com.au**

Printed in China by China Translation & Printing Services.
1 2 3 4 5 6 7 16 15 14 13 12

# Contents

1

# Year 13.

# Congratulations, you have made a great decision!

By choosing to continue your study of English language and literature into NCEA Level 3, you will complete your secondary education with some really useful communication skills.

You have spent several years in your English classroom learning to recognise language techniques and to understand and appreciate how writers use these techniques to achieve specific purposes.

*Achievement English @ Year 13* is designed as a workbook for you to use personally to support your study of English in Year 13. It will assist in the development of your ability to:

- read text with understanding
- analyse text with insight
- express ideas about text with clarity.

*Achievement English @ Year 13* is not a book about assessment. It is designed to help you develop all round as a student of English. However, the exercises we have chosen keep NCEA internal and external Achievement Standards in mind.

We are confident that
you are ready to begin,
so let's get going . . .



ISBN 9780170233293

# Year 13 is different

## English counts

Next year you will be moving into tertiary education or training, or starting your first full-time job. The most desirable general skills for all students and employees are communication skills.

The ability to listen carefully, to write well and to speak effectively is important.

The ability to analyse and research is also very important.

If you can …

- **understand** the issues,
- **gather** useful information,
- **sort out** what is valuable and what is irrelevant
- and **offer** sound opinions based on appropriate information,

… then you will be more successful, whatever path you take in your life.

Studying English will help you to achieve these skills and assist your next step, whether it's into a job or tertiary education.

Add your own **jottings, notes, ideas** from class discussions as you work through this book in school or at home.

This book is yours.

**WRITE ON IT!**

ISBN 9780170233293

# 2 Close Reading – learning to analyse significant aspects of unfamiliar text

## Don't Panic!

This Achievement Standard worries some students because it seems a bit of a mystery. Remember you are preparing for it whenever you read a novel, a short story or a poem and look at the way it has been crafted. You can practise the way to approach an unfamiliar text and this is what we are setting out to do in this part of *Achievement English @ Year 13*.

This book *prepares* you for assessment. It's going to teach you, to remind you about the skills you need to be successful in this assessment. We haven't just chosen easy literature, you might be challenged by some of the material from classic texts. There's plenty of time to read a text over and over, to annotate, to think and to write a response in a 60 minute assessment.

Most of us need a method to approach this Standard successfully. If you approach an unfamiliar text without a method and without having practised that method, you are unlikely to pass. But if you have a method, and you have practised using it regularly then you will pass with flying colours! We know this to be true ...

We also know that lots of students begin by thinking 'I can't do this one' but if that's you, then you are wrong!

It's not scary, it's not difficult.
What it is, is Achievable –
with Merit or Excellence!



ISBN 9780170233293

# Check it!

Let's just assure ourselves that you have the basics.

## Things to do with prose ...

This extract is taken from *The Voyage*, a short story by Katherine Mansfield. Read it carefully, at least twice, and think about what the writer is intending to achieve with her writing. When you have read the passage, find at least one example of each listed feature or term.

| Adjectives | Ellipsis | Oxymoron | Simile |
|---|---|---|---|
| Adverb | Listing | Personification | Effective syntax |
| Alliteration | Onomatopoeia | Repetition | Verbs |

The Picton boat was due to leave at half-past eleven. It was a beautiful night, mild, starry, only when they got out of the cab and started to walk down the Old Wharf that jutted out into the harbour, a faint wind blowing off the water ruffled under Fenella's hat, and she put up her hand to keep it on. It was dark on the Old Wharf, very dark; the wool sheds, the cattle trucks, the cranes standing up so high, the little squat railway engine, all seemed carved out of solid darkness. Here and there on a rounded wood-pile, that was like the stalk of a huge black mushroom, there hung a lantern, but it seemed afraid to unfurl its timid, quivering light in all that blackness; it burned softly, as if for itself.

Fenella's father pushed on with quick, nervous strides. Beside him her grandma bustled along in her crackling black ulster; they went so fast that she had now and again to give an undignified little skip to keep up with them. As well as her luggage strapped into a neat sausage, Fenella carried clasped to her her grandma's umbrella, and the handle, which was a swan's head, kept giving her shoulder a sharp little peck as if it too wanted her to hurry ... Men, their caps pulled down, their collars turned up, swung by; a few women all muffled scurried along; and one tiny boy, only his little black arms and legs showing out of a white woolly shawl, was jerked along angrily between his father and mother; he looked like a baby fly that had fallen into the cream.

ISBN 9780170233293

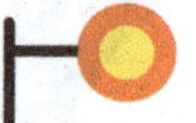

# Things to do with poetry ...

This is a poem by Rhian Gallagher. Read the poem carefully and then complete the task that follows.

Find, highlight and annotate as many examples of the following as you can:

| Alliteration | Repetition |
|---|---|
| Simile | Cliché |
| Metaphor | Senses |
| Onomatopoeia | |

## Under the Pines

Their fine green packed in to make a dark
and this drew me on
round the lagoon. Paddocks open, swept with sunlight
and the pines
serious as a church.

I still hear their boughs
creaking like steps on stairs in depths of night.
Closer in the needles clarified
and the sound became a mast that might not hold.

To walk off the edge of the green world
and into their dust bowl,
that crypt-like half-shadowed temperature,
and once again
to stand there.

Resin scent rinsed like a sharp shower, tingled long after.
Not moving an inch,
myself to myself become a mystery.

*Rhian Gallagher*



ISBN 9780170233293

4

# Close Reading – let's recap the basics

As a student in Year 13 English you bring with you a wealth of knowledge that you have acquired over several years of study. You read, you listen, you watch with understanding. You have learnt to recognise and appreciate good writing. At this level you are learning to use your knowledge, develop it a little further and apply it to more sophisticated text in an assessment situation.

## You will be expected to:

- Respond critically to at least one of each of the following text types:
  - Prose, e.g. persuasive, journalistic, literary
  - Poetry.
- Respond critically to both ideas and language features in unfamiliar texts.
- Communicate ideas and comments clearly and coherently.
- Answer questions that will require short and/or extended written responses.

ISBN 9780170233293

# Close reading prose and poetry

When you 'close read' a piece of writing, whether it is prose or poetry, you are using not only the understanding you have about the content of the piece but also your knowledge of the way writing works. In an assessment of your close reading skills you will be asked to demonstrate your ability to respond to what is written by applying both your knowledge and your response to the text in the answers that you write.

## Approaching a passage for close reading

1. Organise your time to give all the questions your calm attention – avoid last minute rushed responses.
2. Always read the whole passage or poem at least twice before you begin so that you can look for the message or purpose of the whole passage.
3. Ask yourself what type of text it is – oral? written? fiction? non-fiction?
4. Think about each answer before you begin to write. Short purposeful responses are much better than long, rambling ones – and they save time in an assessment situation. Don't confuse short and purposeful with short and generalised.
5. Take note of the title. There are often clues to meaning, mood and angle in the title of the poem or extract.
6. There are also clues in the questions. Read each question very carefully. Unpack it. Highlight (or underline) the key words of instruction and content. Has it got two parts? If so, be sure to answer both clearly. For example:

   *Identify and quote an example of TWO different poetic devices used in the first stanza. Explain the effect created by these.*

   The answer to this question should have **six** parts: a short quotation (perhaps underlining the words signifying the specific device), a label for the device used in the quotation, and an explanation of the effect of the use of the device – times two.

**REMEMBER TO:**

1 Read
2 Think
3 Plan
4 Organise
5 Illustrate



ISBN 9780170233293

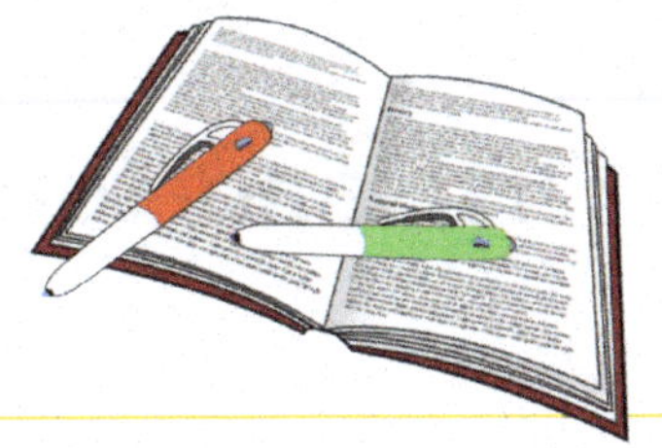

7 Follow the instructions in each question.

- If the question tells you to write **'in your own words'** DO NOT quote from the text.
- If it says **'use specific evidence'** quote the relevant part of the text – not several lines or sentences, hoping that the marker will believe you do know which are the relevant words.
- If it demands that you identify and quote then you must do BOTH.
- If the question asks for one example and you give several, the marker will consider only the first one.
- If the question asks for differences and similarities look for BOTH and organise your answer.

8 Know the terminology. English is no different from other subjects. There is a short-hand of words to describe things. You should KNOW that:

- point of view refers to first, second, third person narration
- syntax means sentence structure
- tense refers to verbs not mood
- infinitive is not the same as imperative and so on …

Remember, the Language Lists on pages 155-163 are designed to remind you of things that you do know but may have forgotten …

9 Explain your answer clearly and to the point. **'Explain the effect'** needs a response that is specific to the passage. Try to avoid weak, generalised responses such as 'it makes it sound interesting' or 'it sticks in your mind'.

10 Illustrate your points with examples.

11 Finally, THE most important thing to do is ANSWER THE QUESTION. If you are aiming for Excellence you will need to make sure that your answers not only discuss features of language used but also consider how they contribute to the overall tone, impact, purpose etc of the passage.

ISBN 9780170233293

# First and foremost

The whole of this book has one simple, fundamental premise ...

... that you will read the text more than once!

Let's remind you why:

## Simple/initial reading

The first time you read a text, whether it is a passage or a poem, an article or a column, a novel, short story or play, you read for meaning and understanding. You follow the ideas or the argument, the description or basic progression of the text. You begin to comprehend its content, you understand the piece as a whole entity and you react, perhaps with curiosity, or interest or intrigue or amusement and you allow yourself to explore, to think about its subject.

## Close/analytical reading

When you read the text again, you read to look for and think about its style and effectiveness. Being aware of your understanding of the content and reactions to it, you begin to assess HOW the passage has presented these ideas and prompted these reactions. You interpret, evaluate and discuss the methods the passage uses to convey its meaning.


ISBN 9780170233293

## The essentials

The essential elements of successful close reading are:

- understanding the question fully

  and

- understanding the text fully.

You will remember that these are the basic questions that you should be able to answer about any text that you are evaluating, whether it be familiar, unfamiliar, prose, poetry, oral or visual.

### 1 What is it about?

Essentially this question is asking for an explanation of the subject or topic of a piece.

But what is it *really* about?

In the study of English the word 'theme' or idea is often used, too. Your answer should look more deeply at the text. For example, a short story might be 'about' an old man robbed on his way home, but on a deeper level its theme might be the collapse of a society's values.

### 2 What is its purpose?

This question wants to know what (you think) the author's intention is. Purpose can be divided simply into categories like:

- To persuade
- To entertain
- To promote an action or thought
- To inform
- To amuse.

But often there is more than one purpose behind a text. Writers sometimes want to change the way we see things, want to make familiar things seem new.

### 3 What is its tone?

You will have the clues to the tone of the text through things like the writer's choice of words and sentence structure (syntax).

But, you may be asked about the writer or director's style. The choice of vocabulary, sentence structure and figurative language creates the style of a text and parts of a text. It may be a passage from a sci-fi novel with much jargon and action or a poem about a child's world, full of imagery and descriptive detail.

### 4 Who is the intended audience?

Where written text is concerned 'audience' means readers.

This question wants to know what kind of person you think the piece has been written for.

But, some things can appeal to different audiences on different levels. A novel like *The Lion, the Witch and the Wardrobe* can be read by a child for its adventure story and by an adult for its religious imagery/references.

ISBN 9780170233293

# Effective annotation

Annotation is a key skill to being efficient in your analysis of text, whether it be as part of your study of a piece of literature or an extract for close reading. In fact, annotation is something that you will use in all your studies, whether at school, university or training for a job. It helps you as you work to completely understand what you read.

## We would expect you to do the following:

**Read** a passage/poem quietly to yourself (or listen to the teacher read it aloud).

**Read it again** and:

- Check you understand the vocabulary. Do you know what all the words mean?
- Highlight words you don't understand and use a dictionary to give you clear, appropriate meanings
- Write these definitions on the page

**Read it again** (yes, a third time!) annotating key features:

- Figurative language like similes and metaphors
- Effective words or phrases
- Special sentence structures


ISBN 9780170233293

- ◯ Details that may answer specific questions
- ◯ Links between different parts of the text
- ◯ Anything you see as interesting/ important
- ◯ Think about the tone created in the passage. How is it created?
- ◯ Is there a particular style? How is it created?
- ◯ What do these things add to your understanding?

## What to do with the annotations

After this 'technical read', look at how these things you have noted work for the passage as a whole. Are they building an image or a character? Is a setting being created? Are they revealing to you a specific mood or atmosphere? Are they persuading you? Making you laugh?

These detailed, annotated notes will create the basis of any discussion or written work you are asked to do on a text.

ISBN 9780170233293

## Putting all this into practice

Use all of these suggestions to help you fully understand and appreciate the following text. It is an extract from *Third Degree*, a novel by Tania Roxborogh. Read it carefully, at least twice, and think about what the writer is intending to achieve with her writing.

### Fire and Ice

When they ask me, I say I cannot remember. But, in my dreams, I am breathless with laughter running down the hall with someone chasing me. I will be caught soon. I am running into the lounge, I grab a hold of the kitchen door, the panelled door; cream, with scrubbed out paint on the edge. My fingers lock into the lip of one panel and I glance quickly back down the lit hall. The others are coming. I laugh, and using the door, and my fingers, I swing, I sweep around toward the kitchen.

I see grey and feel my cheek and top lip crush into grey. Hard, metal grey. I see stars and then the burning starts and my eyes are squeezed tight so the pain cannot get into them but the heat scratches my face, my hair. Rough hands pull me and I hear cries and calls and voices from under water and I am standing in the middle of the living room now.

A child is screaming and screaming somewhere but, when I look, the other children are silent. I hear the screaming but I can only make sounds in my head because it hurts so much. Mum is speaking to me but I don't hear her words. I only sense her fear and see her bravery as she takes my pants off, my socks off, my shirt off.

But, I call to her in my head, but Mum, the boys will see me naked. They will see me. Mum doesn't hear because she is mouthing sounds as she carries me to the bathroom and into the bath.

On the outside, the water is ice-cold but on the inside, it burns and burns and I want to get out. I try to get out but big rough, big sore hands are holding me down. Hot and cold. Heat and ice. Burning and freezing.

"Please let me out", the sound comes out of my mouth. "I would like to get out now", I say politely knowing that manners will always get me places. So, I am out. Shivering from the heat and the cold. Shivering. Shaking. Silently shivering and shaking as I am taken back to the kitchen.



ISBN 9780170233293

I spy a grey metal pot and spilt water; its fire has already seeped away into the floor, leaving only a wet trail. Mum opens the oven door while Dad talks on the phone. "Come closer", she says.

"I can't", I croak, my lips wrestling with me; my cheeks stubbornly refusing to move. "I'm hot". But I am still shaking so they ignore me and pull me closer to the heat. The wave of oven-heat reaches out its scratchy hand and strokes me, rips me and I bleed clear drops onto the bare floor.

*Tania Roxborogh*

**First ...**

Annotate the extract looking for examples of:

- Alliteration
- Metaphor
- Passive verb
- Repetition
- Contrasting words
- Minor sentence
- Personal pronoun
- Simile
- Effective verbs
- Oxymoron
- Personification.

**Now answer these straightforward questions in as much detail as possible. Use quotations and references to the text to support your ideas.**

1 What do you know about the narrator from this passage? Support your answer with evidence from the text.

2 What techniques has the author used to create the sense of panic and pain in the passage?

ISBN 9780170233293

## Digging deeper

This is a famous poem, possibly one of the most extensively studied in the English language. It was written by William Blake in 1794 before we knew much about exotic wild animals. Does spelling the word 'tiger' as *tyger* make it seem even more ancient and mysterious? You will easily find Blake's original, illustrated version of this poem on the Internet.

### The Tyger

Tyger Tyger burning bright,
In the forests of the night;
What immortal hand or eye
Could frame thy fearful symmetry?

In what distant deeps or skies
Burnt the fire of thine eyes?
On what wings dare he aspire?
What the hand, dare seize the fire?

And what shoulder, & what art,
Could twist the sinews of thy heart?
And when thy heart began to beat
What dread hand? & what dread feet?

What the hammer? what the chain,
In what furnace was thy brain?
What the anvil? what dread grasp
Dare its deadly terrors clasp?

When the stars threw down their spears
And watered heaven with their tears:
Did he smile his work to see?
Did he who made the Lamb make thee?

Tyger Tyger burning bright,
In the forests of the night:
What immortal hand or eye,
Dare frame thy fearful symmetry?

*William Blake*


ISBN 9780170233293

### First …

Annotate the poem looking for examples of:

- Alliteration
- Effective imagery
- Metaphor/Personification
- Repetition
- Rhetorical questions
- Rhyme
- Rhythm
- Significant pronouns
- Symbolism.

This poem rhymes. Count the syllables in each line and work out the rhyme pattern. Your teacher may show you how this poem is written in a (mostly) trochaic rhythm. We do not look at analysing rhythm (scansion) in depth because most students will not meet it in class. However, you can look it up on the Internet. We even found a website where you can identify rhythm patterns online http://prosody.lib.virginia.edu/.

**When you think you understand the meaning of the poem, answer the following questions in as much detail as possible. Use quotations and references to the text to support your ideas.**

1 In the first verse why does the tiger burn bright?

___

___

2 How many questions does the poet ask? Are they linked?

___

___

3 In verse 4 what image does the poet use for the creator of the tiger? Why?

___

___

___

___

4 What does he finally want to know? Think about what the words 'he' and 'Lamb' represent in religious imagery. (Look it up if you don't know.)

___

___

___

___

___

___

___

___

___

___

___

ISBN 9780170233293

# Scaffolding an answer

The end result of much of your close reading at this level is to have ideas to offer in a class discussion or answer questions – usually in writing.

Involving yourself in class discussion is an excellent way to improve your understanding of a text. We do appreciate, though, that writing answers to questions is usually where your results come from, so let's think about the question for a moment.

The most important thing is make sure that you understand what the question is asking you to write. After all, there isn't much point filling up the allocated lines but not actually giving the information the examiner requires.

*Achievement English @ Year 13* continues to help develop your strategies for close reading unfamiliar text.

You have written answers to what are commonly called 'scaffolded questions'. You will recollect that a scaffold is a support structure, usually around a building being developed. However, when talking about a scaffolded question in English it refers to a question that offers you support, or hints, as to how to answer the question. Such a question will demand a longer, more detailed and self-structured answer.

This takes more effort, especially in planning your answer.

You understand that scaffolded questions will not ask about an isolated technique or meaning or purpose. Instead, they will ask a wider question but will give you ideas about how to answer them in depth and detail. Always use the clues to complete your answer as fully as possible.

## So what does this mean?

- Instead of being given several short, specific questions you are given one or two more general questions.
- These questions demand a longer, more structured answer.
- At Year 13 you will usually be expected to plan the structure of your response yourself. There may be clues/key words in the question itself to guide you.

## Is that important?

- Your answer will be assessed as N, A, M or E depending on the detail in the response you provide.
- Show that you have heeded what you have learned about longer answers in previous years by planning your answer carefully.
- Your aim is a response that clearly expresses your understanding of the text.



ISBN 9780170233293

## Here is an example of the kind of question we are talking about:

*Explain how the writer develops a sense of chaos. Refer to specific techniques from the text to support your answer.*

This question directs you to a specific idea in the text but requires you to select for yourself appropriate language techniques (more than one is required) to comment on.

## How do you tackle this kind of question?

### Like any other question you are asked!

You are very familiar with answering very specific short questions relating to text. *Why is the word 'xxx' used? What does this metaphor suggest?* etc. You have also had considerable experience of longer, more holistic questions by now.

As with any other question, the key thing is that you actually answer the question. Writing an answer of sufficient length is probably not an issue, but getting enough depth and detail might be something you need to work on.

**Use this strategy to help you**

- ○ Read the question twice.
- ○ Underline key words.
- ○ Read and re-read the passage.
- ○ Underline or highlight detail that looks important to you as you go.
- ○ Make annotations to help you find appropriate parts of the passage or techniques you have noticed easily.
- ○ Take the time to plan your answer. Think of it as a small essay.
- ○ Make sure you are using specific language terminology.
- ○ Check that you always support any point you make with an example.
- ○ Write your answer.
- ○ Re-read your answer – have you answered the question?

ISBN 9780170233293

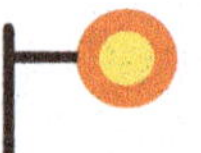

# Practising your skills

In this next section we are going to look at two methods of approaching a text.

| METHOD 1 | METHOD 2 |
|---|---|
| A series of questions focussed on different aspects of the poem. | A general question where you scaffold the structure of a longer answer yourself. |

Both these methods require you to have closely read and understood the whole poem or passage.

Before you go any further let's look at the poem we will base this comprehension on, *Dissection* by Colin Rowbotham.

A poet often writes from his or her own experiences. This poem was written by a student about your age to examine an experience in a school science class. You may find that you can appreciate his experience, especially if you have been in a similar position.

The poem is easy to understand. Read it aloud and it will sound like someone speaking his thoughts aloud. Think about the way the poet shows you what he is doing and then invites you to follow his thoughts to wonder at what he discovers, and then to his conclusion about the point of his learning.

Remember, before you answer any questions you should have read the poem at least three times and made relevant annotations.

### First ...

- Where does the poet appeal to some of your senses?
- Identify the similes and metaphors the poet has used and their effect.
- Suggest reasons why some of the lines are short and why some words are placed out of usual grammatical sequence.
- Think about why punctuation marks are used.
- Look for onomatopoeia, assonance, imperative, alliteration, analogy.

Using what you have now observed about the poem you should be able to write detailed answers to the questions.



ISBN 9780170233293

## Dissection

This rat looks like it is made of marzipan,
Soft and neatly packaged in its envelope;
I shake it free,
Fingering the damp, yellow fur, I know
That this first touch is by far the worst.
There is a book about it that contains
Everything on a rat, with diagrams
Meticulous, but free from blood
Or all the yellow juices
I will have to pour away.
Now peg it out:
My pins are twisted and the board is hard
But, using force and fracturing its legs,
I manage though
And crucify my rat.
From the crutch to the throat the fur is ripped
Not neatly, not as shown in the diagrams,
But raggedly;
My hacking has revealed the body wall
As a sack that is fat with innards to be torn
By the inquisitive eye
And the hand that strips aside.
Inside this taut elastic sack is a surprise;
Not the chaos I had thought to find,
No oozing mash; instead of that
A firmly coiled discipline
Of overlapping liver, folded gut;
A neatness that is like a small machine –
And I wonder what it is that has left this rat,
Why a month of probing could not make it go again,
What it is that has disappeared ...
The bell has gone; it is time to go for lunch.
I fold the rat, replace it in its bag,
Wash from my hands the sweet
Smell of meat and formalin
And go and eat a meat pie afterwards.
So, for four weeks or so, I am told,
I shall continue to dissect this rat;
Like a child
Pulling apart a clock he cannot mend.

*Colin Rowbotham*

ISBN 9780170233293

## Method 1:

1 What is the poet inviting the reader to do in this poem?

2 How does the poet appeal to the reader's senses?

3 Explain to what effect several literary techniques are used in the poem.



ISBN 9780170233293

4 Examine the theme of the poem as revealed in the final three lines.

5 What is your opinion of this theme?

ISBN 9780170233293

## Method 2:

*Discuss the language techniques used in the poem. Why are they important features of the work?*

If you are given a single question requiring a longer answer to respond to you might use a grid like this as a planning device (a scaffold) after you have read the poem, thought about it and completed your annotations. A plan can lead to a more carefully constructed response.

### Plan:

| | |
|---|---|
| **Idea 1** | personal pronouns, imperative |
| **Idea 2** | simile and metaphor |
| **Idea 3** | alliteration, onomatopoeia, assonance |
| **Idea 4** | emotive words – especially verbs and adverbs |

### Sample grid for Idea 1:

| Topic | Example | Description/ deconstruction | Explanation | Evaluation |
|---|---|---|---|---|
| Personal pronouns | 'I shake it free'<br>'I know that this first touch …'<br>'I manage though and crucify'<br>'I had thought' | Describes the narrator's actions.<br>Leads reader through the events and introduces narrator's thoughts. | Structures the poem chronologically and focuses on the personal actions and response of the narrator. | Works well. Understand he is not proficient, dislikes the task but is nevertheless completing it and being provoked into thought by it. |
| Imperatives | 'I am told'<br>'Now peg it out' | Suggests a situation of compulsion. | Tells reader the setting of the poem – a classroom. | |

### Sample paragraph based on these ideas:

In *Dissection* Colin Rowbotham uses the first person pronoun 'I' to lead the reader through the action of the poem. 'I shake it free', 'I know/That this first touch is by far the worst'. We can follow the dissection of the rat and the poet's poor skills as he describes his imperfect actions and his feelings. 'I manage and crucify my rat', 'not the chaos I had thought to find'.

'Now peg it out' is an instruction, clearly putting the actions into a classroom setting. He is following a teacher's directions, doing what he is told to do, not what he wants to do. These techniques work well because the reader understands that the narrator is not proficient and that he dislikes this task that he is obliged to complete.


ISBN 9780170233293

## Have a go:

Choose one of the other ideas listed in the plan on page 26 and complete the grid below.

| Topic | Example | Description/ deconstruction | Explanation | Evaluation |
|---|---|---|---|---|
| | | | | |

Now write your own paragraph/s based on these ideas:

ISBN 9780170233293

# 5 Text type 1: Prose

You should know by now that a 'prose' text is anything that is written that is not poetry. You will be expected to examine an infinite variety of prose text – from a novel to a blog to a ... The techniques writers use are the same, to achieve that variety of outcomes. You know that you have to read a text more than once, you know lots of terminology to express your analysis well.

## Terminology you should be confident with ...

You are in your final year of studying prose at school and by now you know it is important to include the technical language of English in your answer. The list below is what we would expect you to know at this level.

You will notice in the left hand margin there are two circles labelled 'I know' and 'I need to check'. Read through the list and tick the box that best describes your knowledge of each literary term. Look up all the ones you don't know in the Language Lists at the end of this book.

| I know | I need to check | |
|---|---|---|
| ○ | ○ | Abstract noun |
| ○ | ○ | Adjective |
| ○ | ○ | Adverb |
| ○ | ○ | Alliteration |
| ○ | ○ | Allusion |
| ○ | ○ | Assonance |
| ○ | ○ | Cliché |
| ○ | ○ | Collective noun |
| ○ | ○ | Colloquial language |
| ○ | ○ | Common noun |
| ○ | ○ | Comparative adjective |
| ○ | ○ | Conjunction |
| ○ | ○ | Connotation |

| I know | I need to check | |
|---|---|---|
| ○ | ○ | Denotation |
| ○ | ○ | Emotive language |
| ○ | ○ | Euphemism |
| ○ | ○ | Extended metaphor |
| ○ | ○ | Hyperbole |
| ○ | ○ | Imagery |
| ○ | ○ | Irony |
| ○ | ○ | Jargon |
| ○ | ○ | Metaphor |
| ○ | ○ | Narrative voice |
| ○ | ○ | Noun |
| ○ | ○ | Onomatopoeia |
| ○ | ○ | Parts of speech |

| I know | I need to check | |
|---|---|---|
| ○ | ○ | Personification |
| ○ | ○ | Preposition |
| ○ | ○ | Pronoun |
| ○ | ○ | Pun |
| ○ | ○ | Repetition |
| ○ | ○ | Rhetorical question |
| ○ | ○ | Sentence construction |
| ○ | ○ | Simile |
| ○ | ○ | Slang |
| ○ | ○ | Superlative |
| ○ | ○ | Syntax |
| ○ | ○ | Tense |
| ○ | ○ | Verb |


ISBN 9780170233293

We thought we would remind you about:

## Denotation/connotation

Denotation is the dictionary meaning of a word. Connotation is the implied or suggested meaning. For example, the word 'mother' denotes one who has given birth. However the word 'mother' may have the connotation of female, caring, sensible, loving, practicality, experience, homemaker and so on.

**Why?** Because writers choose their vocabulary extremely carefully and they often expect their reader to understand the connotations of the words they choose. They expect their reader to work with them and to bring a certain level of understanding of the connotations of the words they use.

## Extended metaphor

An extended metaphor takes an idea and develops it through a passage or poem.

**Why?** Because there will be some in the literature you study this year – without question!

## Emotive language

Emotive language is the deliberate use of words to exaggerate, describing a subject or an event to interest the reader or listener in a way that will excite the emotions.

Emotive words are used extensively in persuasive writing and speaking to convince others of an author's point of view, often on a controversial issue. They express bias, a tendency towards a particular point of view or preference.

**Why?** Because writers are trying to get a response from their readers and the ones who do this most successfully will be the ones who are chosen for you to study this year.

## Syntax

Syntax is the arrangement, organisation and relationship of words, phrases and clauses in sentences.

**Why?** Because writers, especially those writing fiction, tend to use syntax for purposes other than conveying information and sometimes break the 'rules' quite deliberately for effect.

For revision of syntax see pages 142-154.

ISBN 9780170233293

## The language of prose

To sum up, this chart draws together all of the terminology you will use as you close read prose. Use it as a reference whenever you look at a piece of unfamiliar prose text.

### HOW DO WE APPROACH A PIECE OF UNFAMILIAR PROSE?

**WHAT IS IT ABOUT?**
Explanation of the subject or topic of a piece. Is it a work of fact or fiction? About a place? A character? An event? An object? What are the ideas contained within the text?

**WHAT IS ITS PURPOSE?**
To persuade? To entertain? To amuse? To inform? To discourage the intended audience or promote an action or thought? What is its theme/message?

**WHAT IS ITS TONE?**
Serious, persuasive, angry, humorous, emotive?

**WHO IS THE INTENDED AUDIENCE?**
Who is it aimed at? What age? Gender? Ethnicity? Special interest group?

**How do we tell this?**
**We look at HOW it is written**

**WORDS**

**VOCABULARY**
- Simple
- Complex
- Jargon
- Colloquial
- Slang
- Compound words
- Contractions

**PARTS OF SPEECH**
- Noun
- Pronoun
- Adjective
- Adverb
  - comparative
  - superlative
- Verb
  - tense
- Voice (active/passive)
- Conjunction
- Preposition
- Interjection

**SYNTAX**
(Word Order / Sentences)

**PUNCTUATION**
- Use of . , ? !
- Colon
- Semicolon
- Parentheses (brackets)
- Dash
- Hyphen
- Inverted commas or Quotation marks
- Ellipses

**CONSTRUCTION**
- Minor
- Simple
- Compound
- Complex
- Compound-complex
- Short
- Long

**PATTERNS**
Repetition of:
- phrasing
- sentence structure

**LANGUAGE**

**FIGURATIVE**
- Imagery
- Simile
- Metaphor
  - extended
- Personification
- Euphemism
- Pun
- Cliché
- Symbol
- Hyperbole
- Rhetorical question

**SOUND EFFECTS**
- Alliteration
- Assonance
- Consonance
- Onomatopoeia
- Rhythm
- Rhyme
  - end
  - internal
  - eye

LANGUAGE LIST

**Together these help to give us an OVERALL UNDERSTANDING**



ISBN 9780170233293

# Let's look at a writer's use of techniques

This is the opening of the famous novel *The Power and the Glory* by Graham Greene.

Start by looking at the way the passage has been constructed. Highlight any use of effective **adjectives, adverbs, verbs.** Look for **onomatopoeia, alliteration** and **repetition.** Notice how the writer uses **punctuation.**

However, a writer does not set out to incorporate as many 'techniques' as possible in his or her prose. He or she wants you to 'see' what is being described. Here the writer uses third person narration to show the reader a man and a location.

Mr Tench went out to look for his ether cylinder: out into the blazing Mexican sun and the bleaching dust. A few buzzards looked down from the roof with shabby indifference: he wasn't carrion yet. A faint feeling of rebellion stirred in Mr Tench's heart, and he wrenched up a piece of the road with splintering finger-nails and tossed it feebly up at them. One of them rose and flapped across the town: over the tiny plaza, over the bust of an ex-president, ex-general, ex-human being, over the two stalls which sold mineral water, towards the river and the sea. It wouldn't find anything there: the sharks looked after the carrion on that side. Mr Tench went on across the plaza.

He said 'Buenos dias' to a man with a gun who sat in a small patch of shade against a wall. But it wasn't like England: the man said nothing at all, just stared malevolently up at Mr Tench as if he had never had any dealings with the foreigner, as if Mr Tench were not responsible for his two gold bicuspid teeth. Mr Tench went sweating by, past the Treasury which had once been a church towards the quay.

**Answer the following question in as much detail as possible. Use quotations and references to the text to support your ideas.**

What can you tell about this character and the place he is in from these opening lines?

ISBN 9780170233293

# Prose close reading practice

A variety of prose text and accompanying questions are provided in this section to help you practise answering close reading questions.

## Text 1

This passage is an extract from a magazine article called *Our Evolving Language* by Max Cryer. Read the following passage. Look up words you don't know the meaning of and annotate important features (see pages 155-163).

Two strange geographic confusions were introduced by local media into New Zealand English: all Oriental people became referred to as Asians – carelessly disregarding that Asia is not a race but a place which includes eastern Russia, India, Afghanistan, Nepal, Bhutan, Tibet, Philippines … none of them Oriental. And Māori people, although they are Polynesian, became excluded from Polynesia – as in 'Māori and Polynesian', which is rather like saying 'New Zealanders and Cantabrians'.

Employers paying employees often changed to contractors paying contractees, but who were referred to as 'contractors' – making some confusion about who was paying whom.

More Māori words have moved into the vernacular and everyday reportage. In 2001 an Australian journalist visiting New Zealand wrote with surprise that he needed a dictionary to read the daily newspaper because so many Māori words were in everyday use.

But enlargement of vocabulary hasn't necessarily meant that New Zealand English has become more polished in its usage. Many believe teaching the basics of the English language have been sidelined – school exams can now even accept text spelling as correct, as long as the meaning is clear. To many, this seems we can now feel the heat of the approaching handbasket, as hell gets closer.

Perhaps these are some of the reasons why there are constant cries about the New Zealand standard lack of expression. Captains of industry have difficulty spelling, politicians stumble and mispronounce. Signwriters and journalists use that, which and who as if they all meant the same thing and have abandoned any distinction between less and fewer.

A New Zealand cabinet minister came back from a high-level conference in Europe and commented that his equivalents over there moved easily through two or even three languages 'while we were struggling with just one'. Leaders of professions, television presenters and even the prime minster



ISBN 9780170233293

are convinced that the plural of woman is woman.

A busy office can operate without any phone books. An encyclopaedia is no longer a must-have in many households – nor a dictionary. Just use the computer. The University of Auckland (40,000 students) now requires that all entrants without exception sit a test called Diagnostic English Language Needs Assessment. The Post Office has dramatically reduced its letter collections – there are now so few to collect. It could be said we are losing a connection to print – and consequently to literacy.

Even if so, New Zealand English manages to continue doing a language's job – it communicates.

Whatever its future, the daily exchange of New Zealand English retains some rugged individuality. Words from other languages are absorbed without stress: Diwali, feng shui, pizza, perestroika, sushi. Sports players in their late thirties with a university degree and four children are (rather strangely!) called 'boys' and 'girls'. What we call 'whitebait' bears no relationship to the English fish it is named after. Our 'flax' is a mistaken name given to a plant which has no connection with the real flax from which linen is made. Our 'public schools' are what they say they are – for the public.

And we keep things up to the mark with words of our very own. Where would we be without 'perkbusters' and 'whistleblowers'?

**Answer the following questions in as much detail as possible. Use quotations and references to the text to support your ideas.**

1 The writer contends that NZ English (NZE) is geographically incorrect. In what ways?

2 How has Māori enlarged NZE vocabulary in recent years?

3 What does the underlined sentence mean?

4 What is the cliché being manipulated in paragraph 4? Why is it used?

ISBN 9780170233293

5 Highlight the examples used to show evidence of poor use of NZE. Is there a link?

6 What, does the writer claim, has replaced the dictionary?

7 What does 'rugged individuality' mean in terms of NZE?

8 Give examples of this 'rugged individuality'.

9 Why is 'rather strangely' in brackets and with an exclamation mark?

10 Overall do you think this writer is in favour of the changes he says are happening to NZE?

ISBN 9780170233293

## Text 2

Read the following passage. Look up words you don't know the meaning of and annotate important features (see pages 155-163).

# Zero tolerance on holiday roads? What a good idea

DAVID HILL

Drive carefully, says the protagonist at the end of Aldous Huxley's The Genius and the Goddess. "This is a Christian country and it's the Saviour's birthday. Practically everybody you see will be drunk."

Last month, Transport Minister Paul Swain indicated he wanted to censor the great Kiwi Christmas Story of celebration – inebriation – regurgitation. He proposed *a raft (called a raft because rafts drift directionlessly)* of tough, pre-Christmas road safety measures, including a cut to the legal blood-alcohol level, and targeting of drink-drive teenagers.

The usual *howls of* protest rose. The usual *melee of metaphors* formed. *"A second kick in the teeth,"* claimed a *spokesthing* for the Hospitality Association who also claimed that this Government needs to *pull its head in*. It's true such a cranial retraction would reduce one's chances of being *kicked in the molars,* but that's another story.

Rural objections were heard as well. I don't know much about country life: to me, the country is that bit I dash across to get from the front door to the car door. But I couldn't help being impressed by the farmers' assertions that any threat to their getting *legless in the local* was also a threat to all that is *sacred in our society.*

Like them, I wasn't impressed by Paul Swain's proposals, however. For different reasons, though – I felt they didn't go far enough.

For example, why should we be showing zero tolerance only towards teenagers who drink and drive. *We should have zero tolerance of all teenage activities, including their metabolic processes.* But that's another story, too.

I concede that summer holidays are not an easy time for drivers, who suddenly find themselves on highways *wherecarsarejammedtogetherlikethis.*

But since *'tis the season to curb folly,* and since there are no liberals behind steering wheels, I suggest we extend Mr Swain's intolerance to a degree that would send the Minister of Transport *into transports.*

I'd like to show zero tolerance *to the drivers* of bloke-built holiday homes, especially those which should be preceded by flashing lights and OVERSIZE signs. I want these decent law-abiding folks victimised for two reasons.

First, having worked hard all their lives and now enjoying their totally deserved retirement, they're in absolutely no hurry to get anywhere and can't see why any other driver should be. Second, when they congregate in their holiday-homes-away-from-home *parks, these owners of ROMAN FREE, WAI WORRI and BUG_IT_F_I_NO inevitably start lamenting the decline of literacy and spelling in today's schools.*

I want zero tolerance shown towards *certain cyclists.* These include the racy ones who know they're 10 gears above dreary laws, and who clog the highways with scores *of bobbing black bums.*

Then there are the slow, serene Cape Reinga-to-Bluff cyclists, who pull little trolleys behind their bikes and who ride with a smile on their faces, a song on their lips, a melanoma on their ears. These freedom-wheelers exude such fitness, brightness and smugness that I ache to drive straight over their little trolleys.

I would support minimal tolerance, too, for *Auckland drivers* holidaying in the provinces, who return home and declaim incredulously how they went on this road and it was shingle, and then

they had to swerve because there were these cowpats.

Plus the same severity for *provincial* drivers on holiday in Auckland, who suddenly cross three lanes of the Harbour Bridge because Karlie hasn't seen the Waitemata before.

Let's add *courier van* drivers delivering all those parcels that just made or just missed the Christmas feeding frenzy. Specifically, the courier drivers who treat red lights, yellow lines, *black looks* and *white knuckles* as whimsical irrelevancies.

And we'll include the *family cars* with Jarrod, aged 9, sticking his tongue out in the rear window. Jarrod makes my fingers twitch towards my *bonnet mounted Kalashnikov.*

Why stop at half measures? I want zero tolerance of the *senior stationwagon* so low on its rear springs it seems to be preparing for *sub-orbital flight.*

ISBN 9780170233293

You can recognise these offenders by the roof-rack overflowing with holiday gear to the point where following drivers are liable to receive Karlie's Bob-the-Builder beach-towel across their front windscreen.

A variant on such vehicles is the *surfie* wagon, from which fibreglass boards with *fins like flensing spades* protrude a metre from windows. A truckie friend has his own zero tolerance policy towards these: he drives close enough to threaten fin amputations. Needless to say, I can't approve...enough.

Although *we never the Swain shall meet,* let's extend his intolerance to cover vehicles whose occupants *toss takeaway food* or drink containers out of the window; vehicles whose drivers still wear *back-to-front baseball caps;* vehicles *towing trailers* of poorly packed garden rubbish whose *cascading contents* turn SH1 into a bush walk.

In a final flurry of kick-in-the-teeth enthusiasm we'll include cars *with personalised plates* reading ALL MYN, BAD BOI or LUSTI, plus cars towing 10 tons of Beach Belle on a bouncing, swinging, road-obscuring trailer to another harbour where they can *moor it opposite the waterfront pub.*

Oh, and cars full of *lawn bowlers* wearing lawn bowlers' hats, who know it's all right to turn out of side streets in front of oncoming traffic because it's only 50m till they turn off again to their motel.

Around here, I start to sense some Automobilis Anonymous muttering that if I had my way, there'd be nobody allowed on our roads. Well, of course. We all know that the only really safe and competent driver around is us. *While others succumb to road rage, we remain a Road Sage.*

But that's another story. ■

**Answer the following questions in as much detail as possible. Use quotations and references to the text to support your ideas.**

1 The opening paragraph uses a quotation. It juxtaposes two seemingly incongruous ideas. Explain what these are. How does this quotation lead into the article?

2 Identify two personal pronouns used in this article. Explain why each is used. Quote from the text to support your ideas.

3 This article is written for a New Zealand audience. Apart from the use of certain proper nouns, how can you tell?

4 Which groups did not want the suggested new restrictions? What is the writer's attitude towards those who oppose the new road safety measures? How can you tell?



ISBN 9780170233293

5 Comment on the use of cliche, alliteration, hyperbole and allusion in this article.

i

ii

iii

iv

6 Give two examples of the writer using the visual presentation of words to suggest meaning. Explain the meaning of each example.

7 Comment on the use of parentheses in paragraph 2.

8 Comment on the use of demonstratives in paragraph 13, beginning: 'I would support ...'

9 Comment on the use of colours in paragraph 14, beginning: 'Let's add courier ...'

10 In what way does the article differ from what you might expect from its title?

## Text 3

Read the following extract from *Memoirs of a Peon* by Frank Sargeson. It describes a scene in detail involving a poor young man who has become acquainted with the wealthy Gower-Johnson family of Remuera. Look up words you don't know the meaning of and annotate important features (see pages 155-163).

I had not been introduced to Mr Gower-Johnson, but I wondered if I had seen him when I climbed to the lily pool terrace to fetch Mrs Gower-Johnson her favourite parasol which she had left in her favourite clematis-draped summerhouse. A stoutish man, dressed as though for bowls with a waistcoat on underneath his blazer, was standing looking very intently at the pool; and as I passed him I murmured a polite good afternoon without eliciting any sign of a response. But a moment or so later, without removing his eyes from the pool, he called to a workman some distance off – a young man wearing a football jersey who was engaged in weeding one of the many herbaceous borders. I now had the parasol and was again near the pool; and looking too, I saw a frog seated upon one of the lily leaves. It was a somewhat unreal sight: the creature was green, a somewhat lighter shade than the unblemished and perfect leaf it sat upon, but it was so brightly gilded that it might have been a varnished toy in a shop window waiting to be bought for some child. I stopped to watch as the young man approached, and immediately the frog was pointed out to him his hand went to the long sheath-knife he wore on his hip: then he crept swiftly to the rim of the pool from which he suddenly reached out to slash with his knife. The frog disappeared as the water splashed and then bubbled; but just before I turned away the surface was broken by a very tiny frog-hand which looked desperately mute and forlorn as it poked up through the hole where the leaf had been slashed. I ran down the stone steps, and presenting the parasol to Mrs Gower-Johnson I said, "I've just seen a green-and-gold frog sitting on a lily leaf." And she answered, "Oh, have you! They're such a nuisance, they keep us awake at night."



ISBN 9780170233293

**Answer the following questions in as much detail as possible. Use quotations and references to the text to support your ideas.**

1 Explain what the writer shows you about the Gower-Johnsons and about the young male narrator's relationship with the family.

2 Comment on the language the writer chooses to use to describe this scene. What sort of mood is created?

3 What comment do you think the writer is making about these wealthy urban people through this scene? And might there be a message for the young man in the event he has just witnessed?

ISBN 9780170233293

## Text 4

Read the following passage from *Down and Out in Paris and London* by George Orwell. Look up words you don't know the meaning of and annotate important features (see pages 155-163).

Our cafeterie was a murky cellar measuring twenty feet by seven by eight high, and so crowded with coffee-urns, breadcutters and the like that one could hardly move without banging against something. It was lighted by one dim electric bulb, and four or five gas-fires that sent out a fierce red breath. There was a thermometer there, and the temperature never fell below 110 degrees Fahrenheit — it neared 130 at some times of the day. At one end were five service lifts, and at the other an ice cupboard where we stored milk and butter. When you went into the ice cupboard you dropped a hundred degrees of temperature at a single step; it used to remind me of the hymn about Greenland's icy mountains and India's coral strand. Two men worked in the cafeterie besides Boris and myself. One was Mario, a huge, excitable Italian — he was like a city policeman with operatic gestures — and the other, a hairy, uncouth animal whom we called the Magyar; I think he was a Transylvanian, or something even more remote. Except the Magyar we were all big men, and at the rush hours we collided incessantly.

The work in the cafeterie was spasmodic. We were never idle, but the real work only came in bursts of two hours at a time — we called each burst 'UN COUP DE FEU'. The first COUP DE FEU came at eight, when the guests upstairs began to wake up and demand breakfast. At eight a sudden banging and yelling would break out all through the basement; bells rang on all sides, blue-aproned men rushed through the passages, our service lifts came down with a simultaneous crash, and the waiters on all five floors began shouting Italian oaths down the shafts. I don't remember all our duties, but they included making tea, coffee and chocolate, fetching meals from the kitchen, wines from the cellar and fruit and so forth from the dining-room, slicing bread, making toast, rolling pats of butter, measuring jam, opening milk-cans, counting lumps of sugar, boiling eggs, cooking porridge, pounding ice, grinding coffee — all this for from a hundred to two hundred customers. The kitchen was thirty yards away, and the dining-room sixty or seventy yards. Everything we sent up in the service lifts had to be covered by a voucher, and the vouchers had to be carefully filed, and there was trouble if even a lump of sugar was lost. Besides this, we had to supply the staff with bread and coffee, and fetch the meals for the waiters upstairs. All in all, it was a complicated job.

I calculated that one had to walk and run about fifteen miles during the day, and yet the strain of the work was more mental than physical. Nothing could be easier, on the face of it, than this stupid scullion work, but it is astonishingly hard when one is in a hurry. One has to leap to and



ISBN 9780170233293

fro between a multitude of jobs — it is like sorting a pack of cards against the clock. You are, for example, making toast, when bang! down comes a service lift with an order for tea, rolls and three different kinds of jam, and simultaneously bang! down comes another demanding scrambled eggs, coffee and grapefruit; you run to the kitchen for the eggs and to the dining-room for the fruit, going like lightning so as to be back before your toast bums, and having to remember about the tea and coffee, besides half a dozen other orders that are still pending; and at the same time some waiter is following you and making trouble about a lost bottle of soda-water, and you are arguing with him. It needs more brains than one might think. Mario said, no doubt truly, that it took a year to make a reliable cafetier.

**Answer the following question in as much detail as possible. Use quotations and references to the text to support your ideas.**

1 The writer is describing a personal experience in the kitchen of a hotel in Paris. What does he say about the working conditions, the work itself and the qualities required to work there successfully?

**NOTE:** This is a three part question … it requires a three part answer!

ISBN 9780170233293

## Text 5

Read the following passage from *Along Rideout Road That Summer* by Maurice Duggan. Look up words you don't know the meaning of and annotate important features (see pages 155-163).

I'd walked the length of Rideout Road the night before, following the noise of the river in the darkness, tumbling over ruts and stones, my progress, if you'd call it that, challenged by farmers' dogs and observed by the faintly luminous eyes of wandering stock, steers, cows, stud-bulls or milk-white unicorns or, better, a full quartet of apocalyptic horses browsing the marge. In time and darkness I found Puti Hohepa's farmhouse and lugged my fibre suitcase up to the verandah, after nearly breaking my leg in a cattlestop. A journey fruitful of one decision – to flog a torch from somewhere. And of course I didn't. And now my feet hurt; but it was daylight and, from memory, I'd say I was almost happy. Almost. Fortunately I am endowed both by nature and later conditioning with a highly developed sense of the absurd; knowing that you can imagine the pleasure I took in this abrupt translation from shop-counter to tractor seat, from town pavements to back-country farm, with all those miles of river-bottom darkness to mark the transition. In fact, and unfortunately there have to be some facts, even fictional ones, I'd removed myself a mere dozen miles from the parental home. In darkness, as I've said, and with a certain stealth. I didn't consult dad about it, and, needless to say, I didn't tell mum. The moment wasn't propitious; dad was asleep with the Financial Gazette threatening to suffocate him and mum was off somewhere moving, as she so often did, that this meeting make public its whole-hearted support for the introduction of flogging and public castration for all sex offenders and hanging, drawing and quartering, for almost everyone else, and as for delinquents (my boy!) ... Well, put yourself in my shoes, there's no need to go on. Yes, almost happy, though my feet were so tender I winced every time I tripped the clutch.

Almost happy, shouting Kubla Khan, a bookish lad, from the seat of the clattering old Ferguson tractor, doing a steady five miles an hour in a cloud of seagulls, getting to the bit about the damsel with a dulcimer and looking up to see the reputedly wild Hohepa girl perched on the gate, feet hooked in the bars, ribbons fluttering from her ukelele. A perfect moment of recognition, daring rider, in spite of the belch of carbon monoxide from the tin-can exhaust up front on the bonnet. Don't, however, misunderstand me: I'd not have you think we are here embarked on the trashy clamour of boy meeting girl. No, the problem, you are to understand, was one of connexion. How connect the dulcimer with the ukelele, if you follow. For a boy of my bents this problem of how to cope with the shock of the recognition of a certain discrepancy between the real and the written was rather like watching mum with a



ISBN 9780170233293

shoehorn wedging nines into sevens and suffering merry hell. I'm not blaming old STC for everything, of course. After all some other imports went wild too; and I've spent too long at the handle of a mattock, a critical function, not to know that. The stench of the exhaust, that's to say, held no redolence of that old hophead's pipe. Let us then be clear, and don't for a moment, gentlemen, imagine that I venture the gross unfairness, the patent absurdity, the rank injustice (your turn) of blaming him for spoiling the pasture or fouling the native air. It's just that there was this problem in my mind, this profound, cultural problem affecting dramatically the very nature of my inheritance, nines into sevens in this lovely smiling land. His was the genius as his was the expression which the vast educational brouhaha invited me to praise and emulate, tranquillizers ingested in maturity, the voice of the ring-dove, look up though your feet be in the clay.

Of course I understood immediately that these were not matters I was destined to debate with Fanny Hohepa. Frankly, I could see that she didn't give a damn; it was part of her attraction. She thought I was singing. She smiled and waved, I waved and smiled, turned, ploughed back through gull white and coffee loam and fell into a train of thought not entirely free of Fanny and her instrument, pausing to wonder, now and then, what might be the symptoms, the early symptoms, of carbon monoxide poisoning. Drowsiness? Check. Dilation of the pupils? Can't check. Extra cutaneous sensation? My feet. Trembling hands? Vibrato. Down and back, down and back, turning again, Dick and his Ferguson, Fanny from her perch seeming to gather about her the background of green paternal acres, fold on fold. I bore down upon her with all the eager erubescence* of youth, with my hair slicked back. She trembled, wavered, fragmented and reformed in the pungent vapour through which I viewed her. (oh for an open-air job, eh mate?) She plucked, very picture in jeans and summer shirt of youth and suspicion, and seemed to sing. I couldn't of course hear a note. Behind me the dog-leg furrows and the bright ploughshares. Certainly she looked at her ease and, even through the gassed up atmosphere between us, too deliciously substantial to be a creature down on a visit from Mount Abora. I was glad I'd combed my hair. Back, down and back. Considering the size of the paddock this could have gone on for a week. I promptly admitted to myself that her present position, disposition or posture, involving as it did some provocative tautness of cloth, suited me right down to the ground. I mean to hell with the idea of having her stand knee-deep in the thistle thwanging her dulcimer and plaintively chirruping about a pipedream mountain. In fact she was natively engaged in expressing the most profound distillations of her local experience, the gleanings of a life lived in rich contact with a richly understood and native environment: A Slow Boat to China, if memory serves. While I, racked and shaken, composed words for the plaque which would one day stand here to commemorate our deep rapport.

*blushing

ISBN 9780170233293

Before answering the questions on the Maurice Duggan passage read the following extracts from the poem *Kubla Khan* by Samuel Taylor Coleridge (1772–1834).

In Xanadu did Kubla Khan
A stately pleasure-dome decree:
Where Alph, the sacred river, ran
Through caverns measureless to man
Down to a sunless sea.
So twice five miles of fertile ground
With walls and towers were girdled round:
And there were gardens bright with sinuous rills,
Where blossomed many an incense-bearing tree;
And here were forests ancient as the hills
Enfolding sunny spots of greenery.
…
…
A damsel with a dulcimer
In a vision once I saw:
It was an Abyssinian maid,
And on her dulcimer she played,
Singing of Mount Abora.
Could I revive within me
Her symphony and song,
To such a deep delight 'twould win me,
That with music loud and long,
I would build that dome in air,
That sunny dome! Those caves of ice!
And all who heard should see them there,
And all should cry, "Beware! Beware!
His flashing eyes, his floating hair!
Weave a circle round him thrice,
And close your eyes with holy dread,
For he on honey-dew hath fed,
And drunk the milk of Paradise."



ISBN 9780170233293

**Answer the following questions in as much detail as possible. Use quotations and references to the text to support your ideas.**

1 What do you learn about the narrator and his journey from the opening sentence?

2 Comment on the use of the word 'better' in the opening sentence and its link to his comment about a torch.

3 Comment on the syntax of these lines:

*'In time and darkness I found Puti Hohepa's farmhouse and lugged my fibre suitcase up to the verandah, after nearly breaking my leg in a cattlestop. A journey fruitful of one decision – to flog a torch from somewhere. And of course I didn't. And now my feet hurt; but it was daylight and, from memory, I'd say I was almost happy. Almost.'*

4 What is the effect of the use of personal pronouns?

5 What does he think is absurd?

6 How does the passage appeal to the senses? Give three examples from the text and explain each one's effect.

ISBN 9780170233293

7 What are his parents like? What is his relationship with them? Support your answer with evidence from the text.

8 Three phrases have been placed in parentheses. Quote each one and explain why it is in parentheses.

9 Explain the meaning of three of these phrases:

threatening to suffocate him *(line 20/21)*
a bookish lad *(line 28)*
cloud of seagulls *(line 30)*
wedging nines into sevens *(line 41)*
some other imports went wild too *(line 42/43)*
vast educational brouhaha *(line 52)*
green paternal acres *(line 66)*

i

ii

iii

10 Give at least two examples of the use of humour in the passage.

i

ii


ISBN 9780170233293

## Now look at how the second text (*Kubla Khan*) relates to the first.

11 Explain in detail what the young man's 'profound cultural problem' is and how it relates to the lines from the poem that he refers to.

What is the writer suggesting about New Zealand's education system in the middle of the 20th century?

ISBN 9780170233293

## Text 6

Read the following extract from *Cider with Rosie* by Laurie Lee. Look up words you don't know the meaning of and annotate important features (see pages 155-163).

Radiating from that house, with its crumbling walls, its thumps and shadows, its fancied foxes under the floor, I moved along paths that lengthened inch by inch with my mounting strength of days. From stone to stone in the trackless yard I sent forth my acorn shell of senses, moving through unfathomable oceans like a South Sea savage island-hopping across the Pacific. Antennae of eyes and nose and grubbing fingers captured a new tuft of grass, a fern, a slug, the skull of a bird, a grotto of bright snails.

From the harbour mouth of the scullery floor I learned the rocks and reefs and the channels where safety lay. I discovered the physical pyramid of the cottage, its stores and labyrinths, its centres of magic and of the green, sprouting island-garden upon which it stood. My mother and sisters sailed past me like galleons in their busy dresses, and I learned the smells and sounds which followed in their wakes, the surge of breath, carbolic, song and grumble, and smashing of crockery.

The scullery was a mine of all the minerals of living. Here, I discovered water – a very different element from the green crawling scum that stank in the garden tub. You could pump in pure blue gulps out of the ground, you could swing on the pump handle and it came out sparkling like liquid sky. And it broke and ran and shone on the tiled floor or quivered in a jug, or weighted your clothes with cold. You could drink it, draw with it, froth it with soap, swim beetles across it, or fly it on bubbles in the air. You could put your head in it, and open your eyes, and see the sides of the bucket buckle, and hear your caught breath roar, and work your mouth like a fish, and smell the lime from the ground. Substance of magic – which you could wear or tear, confine or scatter, or send down holes, but never burn or break or destroy.

Here too was the scrubbing of floors and boots, of arms and necks, of red and white vegetables. Walk in to the morning disorder of this room and all the garden was laid out dripping on the table. Chopped carrots like copper pennies, radishes and chives, potatoes dipped and stripped clean from their coats of mud, the snapping of tight pea-pods, long shells of green pearls, and the tearing of glutinous beans from their nests of wool.



ISBN 9780170233293

**Answer the following question in as much detail as possible. Use quotations and references to the text to support your ideas.**

1 This passage describes a place from a particular point of view. Explain what the words reveal about the narrator himself and about children in general.

Your answer might include some of these points:

- The narrator's world
- How a child's view is different from an adult's
- How the writer uses images that link together
- How the senses provide close observation of things
- How children learn.

ISBN 9780170233293

## An aside on ... style

When the word style is applied to a text it refers to the features of that text that make it typical of an author, a historical period, a particular audience, a genre or kind of text. For instance:

- a humorous style
- a satirical style
- a serious style
- a scientific style
- a didactic style
- a conversational style
- a persuasive style
- a witty style
- a sarcastic style
- an ironic style.

### Some possible ways to approach a passage in search of its style

**What is the passage about?**

- List or highlight the main ideas/topics.

**What is the tone of the passage?**

- Is it humorous or serious, angry or amusing, satirical or logical? It can be more than one!
- Does it amuse, persuade, inform or entertain you?
- Is it balanced or one-sided? Passionate or dispassionate?
- Is it the writer's own opinion or is there a persona?
- What is the writer's intended effect on the reader?
- What kind of reader is it aimed at?
- What kind of publication is it taken from – a novel? A newspaper? A specialist magazine? A play?

**What is the theme of the passage?**

- Is there a meaning beyond the basic subject of the passage?
- Are there hidden messages?
- Is there a judgement or a conclusion that the writer leads you to?
- Is it stated explicitly or can you infer meanings?

Once you have some opinions about the subject and theme of the writing, who the audience is, what the writer's attitude is towards that subject, you can go on to look at how the piece achieves its style.

### Steps to take

1. What does the **title** tell you?
2. What are the main steps in the **development of the passage's ideas**? Divide the passage into sections.
3. Identify where/how the **sections** are linked, for example, with key words, with similar images, with repeated syntax.
4. Look at the **vocabulary** the writer has chosen. How does it suit the audience, the intention of the piece, the writer's attitude, the tone of the piece. Is the reader involved? How? Look for formal and informal language, for specialised words, for words with connotations, for irony, satire, cynicism, exaggeration for personal pronouns, for neologisms, for slang, for colloquialisms, for allusions to events, or other texts, for personal anecdotes, for figures of speech, for the sound of the words – rhythm, assonance, onomatopoeia, alliteration, etc.
5. Consider **imagery**. Does the piece use imagery (simile, metaphor, personification, litotes, hyperbole, etc)? What for? Symbolism? To suggest or imply meanings or an attitude? To create atmosphere?
6. Look at the **sentence structure**. Short, long or a mixture? Simple or complex? Active or passive? Are there patterns of sentence construction? What conjunctions are used?

Whenever you comment on a passage you are using your knowledge of language devices and your appreciation of how they work to inform your comments on the passage. What you write in response to a question is not naming of parts – to be precise and concise you need the terminology to use to express your ideas with precision.



ISBN 9780170233293

# Something a little different — SATIRE

### What is satire?

Satire is a literary genre where individuals, certain groups of people or society itself are criticised. The vices or shortcomings, bad behaviour or foolishnesses of people are displayed and ridiculed in a way that is usually meant to be funny or humorous but often carries a serious meaning beneath the humour. Satirists seek change; want improvements in the world, therefore their writing can be seen as constructive criticism – especially by those who agree with them.

### What techniques do satirists use?

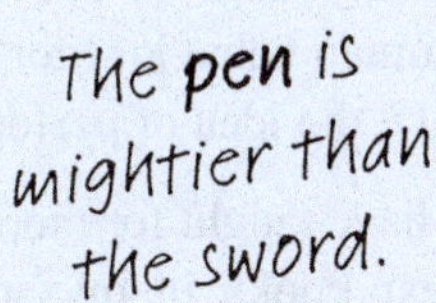


A lot of irony. Irony is a literary technique that says the opposite of what it means. When used for satire, irony pretends to accept, even approve of, what the writer wishes to criticise or attack.

Well-known light-hearted irony currently in New Zealand is shown in the Tui beer billboards. They are designed to be amusing/funny. They say the opposite of what they mean, followed by 'Yeah right' that highlights the irony! But they are also making a comment on something in our society.

**Allusion**

An indirect reference to an event or person. The effect is to extend an image or idea in the listener's mind.

**Analogy**

A similarity between two things that are otherwise different. All metaphors and similes are based on analogy.

**Comparison**

Similarities and/or differences between two people, places, ideas or things are examined.

**Double entendre**

From the French meaning *double meaning.*
A word or phrase that can be interpreted in two ways, especially where one meaning is indelicate.
This type of humour depends on ambiguity. Ambiguity means unclear, imprecise meaning.

**Hyperbole**

Deliberate exaggeration.

**Irony**

The use of words that, when taken in context, are revealed to mean the opposite of what is said.

**Juxtaposition**

Words or phrases are placed side-by-side, especially for comparison or contrast, inviting the reader to make the connection and discover a meaning.

**Parody**

A humorous imitation of another piece of writing or performance. The parody is designed to ridicule the attitudes, style or subject matter of the original.

ISBN 9780170233293

Peter Lyons is a New Zealand teacher. He is writing about performance pay for teachers. Annotate important features of satire (see previous page). Use this passage to approach the four essential questions you should be able to answer on any text.

# Peter Lyons reckons he has what it takes to be the best teacher south of Tokyo.

A key rule of economics is that incentives shape human behaviour for better or worse. I am starting to like the idea of performance pay for teachers.

I have taught for more than 20 years. I have authored text books in my subject and been a lecturer for beginning teachers in commerce.

I think a merit-based system of pay would suit me.

On the first day of my teacher training, the lecturer asked us why we wanted to teach. Many of my fellow students had noble ideals such as wanting to make a difference or share their passion for learning. One woman even said she liked children.

I said I wanted long holidays. But if my pay depended on my performance my attitude would certainly change.

I teach economics, which is an option students can choose to take. If performance pay was introduced the first thing I would do is restrict those students who could take my subject. There will be no low achievers or slackers taking my subject if it costs me money.

This shouldn't be a problem, as the guy who teaches geography is a nice chap and still believes that all students can succeed so he can pick up the leftovers. I feel a bit sorry for those who teach core subjects such as English because they have to teach everyone, but that's their problem for spending their university days reading poetry, drinking cheap cask wine and smoking dubious cigarettes.

There is little point in teaching the less able kids if my pay packet depends on exam results. I'll leave that to the idealistic first-year teachers who believe they can make a difference.

I will drill my students in what they need to know for the exams. It is pretty simple, as NCEA exams are relatively consistent each year. I would demand that students give priority to homework in my subject otherwise they will face endless detentions. I will focus exclusively on the exams. There is no point in teaching students about financial literacy and how to manage money if this is not going to improve their marks and my pay. Show me the money! I love incentives.

Under merit pay I have a great opportunity to be one of the highest paid teachers in New Zealand. I will get my NCEA students to do endless resits of internal assessments until they get it right. I will make them rote learn the answers for the exam until they can repeat them in their sleep. Any student unable to perform this simple cognitive task will be withdrawn from sitting the exam to maintain my excellent pass rates. Nothing will be allowed to interfere with my desire to be the best teacher south of Tokyo. I will earn my nickname of "Monotony Lyons".

I am fortunate to work in a department with innovative and sharing teachers. It's great working with caring and sharing types and for some reason, there seem to be a lot of them in teaching. They tell me about the exciting learning activities they are doing with their students. Each week when I visit the principal to talk about my successes, I will tell him about these innovative teaching methods that I am running with my students.

There is little point in being fantastic in the classroom if no one knows about it.

Each school assembly, notices will be read out announcing that I am running yet another extra-curricula activity. I may have to invent a few imaginary clubs but that doesn't matter as long as people are aware of the vast extent of my contributions to the wider life of the school. I teach at a Catholic boys school. I could set up an Islamic prayer group or a cross stitching club. That would ensure few attendees and little extra work.

I teach the Cambridge international examination system. This is an English franchise that some schools have adopted because of concerns about NCEA. This system allows students to resit at mid-



ISBN 9780170233293

year the next year if they are unhappy with their results. I would insist that all students taking my subject do a resit to improve their previous year's results. This should ensure the cash flows my way.

When exam results are announced at the start of each year and my students do the best, I will humbly rise to my feet in the staffroom. I will announce with suitable humility that examination success is largely the result of student application and ability combined with excellent teaching.

Such success can only be the result of 100 per cent application by teacher and student. I do a fine line in humility when the occasion requires and money is on the line. Merit pay for teachers? Bring it on!

*Peter Lyons*

**Answer the following questions in as much detail as possible. Use quotations and references to the text to support your ideas.**

1 What is the article about?

2 What is its purpose?

3 What is its tone?

4 Who is the intended audience?

ISBN 9780170233293

5 Have a go at writing a satirical piece on performance pay for students!

## Humour and satire go hand in hand

Here's an Australian newspaper columnist having a crack at fashion in the IT world. Read his column, enjoy it, and then ask yourself: why is it funny?

### Light of my life: with buttons and glows, you're not just a pretty fascia

The Unit is great, The Unit is the best: it makes your life so much more happy and rewarding, because all your friends will go "Oh, you have The Unit … yeah, reckon it's all hype … yeah, I'm not into them'' but you know they want one BAD, ha-ha, stupid, envious Unit-less jerks who are my best friends.

The Unit can do magical stuff, but it is not boring magical stuff like flying through the sky or cooking chicken schnitzels that are not too dry. The magicalness of The Unit is its SHINY GLOWY PRETTINESS. The shiny-glowy-prettiness gets even more magical at night, this is when The Unit really comes into its own.



ISBN 9780170233293

The Unit has, like, ultra-maxi-super features. It's got this thing called geo-pudenda 69XPPSTmotion that transports you into a parallel-multiverse according to quantum-gravitational String Theory, but you have to buy an extra cable for 12 bucks from Dick Smiths, so you'll probably never use it. They never tell you about that extra cable. Cheeky.

If you drive around a lot and you're always getting lost, The Unit can actually give you street directions in your car - it is almost as fast and convenient as opening a directory and looking inside and saying "Turn left'' in your own sexy woman's voice named Audrey. The Unit has loads of fun little games and colourful activities that you can spin, swipe and touch with your fingers - kind of like the games you would find on a Fisher Price Baby Activity Centre with a squeaky ball and spinning rattle, but you would be too embarrassed to play with those because you are 37.

A woman lives inside The Unit, she really does. You can talk to her and say "Do I need an umbrella today?'' or "What is the weather like today?'' and you can keep bugging her with weather questions until you hear weeping, then a funny little blipping noise that may be a gunshot, then she doesn't speak any more.

Whoahhhh, hang on. Before you rush off to buy The Unit, you should know that it costs lots of money, but you can easily go without milk and vegetables for a year. And the buttons on The Unit are soft touchscreen buttons so you won't snap your chalky calcium-deficient finger-bones when you press them.

Do NOT buy the cheap alternative to The Unit, called The Unat, which seems the same, works the same, does everything the same, but it will just not look right when you sit down in a laneway tapas bar and use it to design a graffiti-art flyer for an Afghan Refugee Falafel'n'Fattoush Family Fun-Night Fund-raiser.

The Unit cannot be bought just on its own: you also need to buy chargers, adaptors, connectors, docks, and a cup of coffee from Gloria Jeans so you can sit there for the rest of your life and use the buy-a-coffee free Wi-Fi.

Also it would be a shame to drop The Unit and damage its shiny-glowy-prettiness, so you must buy a jet-black three-ply Kevlar-fibre protector-case. This makes it look a bit like The Unat, but do not worry, people will understand.

You want The Unit, you must have The Unit, your life will become perfect and meaningful and amazing with The Unit, so go on, buy one. Don't worry that The Unit2 comes out next month and it's got more advanced shiny-glowy-prettiness - you can just buy that one. (Also buy The Unit3, which comes out 20 minutes later.)

*Danny Katz*

**Now …**

**Re-read the passage and annotate at least one example of the following:**

- Cliché
- Irony
- Hyperbole
- Superlative
- Allusion
- Pun
- Neologism
- Jargon
- Stereotyping
- Pseudo-scientific terminology
- Simile
- Metaphor
- Repetition
- Contrast
- Comparison
- Colloquial language
- Personal pronoun
- Font variations
- Unusual punctuation
- Sentence structure
- Balance
- Tricolon
- Ellipsis
- Imperative.

**Answer the following questions in as much detail as possible. Use quotations and references to the text to support your ideas.**

1 First of all the writer needs a quirk of human behaviour to focus on. What is it, in this case?

2 Then he needs a personal voice, a tone to suit his topic and his column persona. What is Danny Katz's persona here and what techniques help create that persona?

3 How does he criticise the way the Unit is advertised and sold?

4 How does he criticise the buyers of the Unit?



ISBN 9780170233293

5 What is the tone of this piece?

**Answering the questions above has given you the information to answer a scaffold-type question. You will need to restructure your information to answer this single question appropriately.**

6 What makes this column funny?

You might comment on the persona created by the writer, how he criticises the seller and the buyer and the tone of the column as it comments on human behaviour.

ISBN 9780170233293

# 6 Text type 2: Poetry

If you have been using the *Achievement English* books through your senior schooling, we hope you have grown in confidence in analysing poems and have learnt to enjoy reading poetry.

The beauty of a poem in these classroom and assessment circumstances is that it is a complete piece. There is no guessing what has gone before or what has happened after – the poet has put it all in the one poem.

Poets are deeply interested in words ... in a very few words they evoke emotion, they make us think. Of course it is the specific words they have chosen and the way in which they combine these words that create such powerful effects. That is what you are trying to work out when you analyse poetry. What has the poem made me think and feel? How has it managed to do this?

Because we know that some of you will still be saying 'Urgh' we thought we should repeat the simple advice we have given you previously.

ISBN 9780170233293

## How to approach a poem

1 **Don't worry.** A poem is not a puzzle that must be deciphered completely before you get the 'right' answer.

A poet spends a lot of time choosing exactly the best words for their poem. You may not understand them all or be able to see why they were chosen. That doesn't mean you cannot understand the idea that the poet is trying to share. Some poems you may be asked to read are written by and for people who have a lot more experience of life than you do at the moment. You can enjoy and understand parts of a poem without fully grasping it all.

2 When you study an unfamiliar text in class you may be given the text on a single sheet for annotation. If not, **make one for yourself** and add your own annotations.

3 Always read a poem lots of times. Try to read it aloud. The first poetry was meant to be spoken, or read aloud, just like children's poems and stories. Make sure you read to the punctuation. Often an idea is not contained in each separate line.

4 Decide what you think the poem is generally about. There may be a simple surface meaning and a deeper one, too. Do this before you begin to look at the way the poet has chosen words and images, has used figures of speech and layout, to deliver that meaning. Sometimes the title can hint at the theme of a poem.

5 Look at the poem in more detail. Always ask yourself why the poet chose those particular words. Often you will be asked questions that guide you towards particular things like figures of speech (simile, metaphor, sound devices), parts of speech (nouns, verbs) and pattern (rhythm, rhyme, sentence structure). At this level it is important that you are able to recognise and name the devices used, but much more important that you can comment on their effect in terms of the poem as a whole. Use a dictionary to look up any words you do not understand.

6 Respond. Think about why you enjoyed the poem. Was it humorous? Did it have something important to say? Was it relevant to your life? Poems mean different things to different people. Your personal response may be different from your classmates, but it is just as valid.

7 Don't worry.

Relax and enjoy as much poetry as you can. Read some for pleasure!

ISBN 9780170233293

## Annotating a poem

A useful way of trying to understand and appreciate a poem is to place a copy of it in the middle of a sheet of paper and annotate your ideas around it.

1 Read the poem aloud if possible, or alternatively listen to someone else read it.

2 Read the poem to yourself several more times as you get confident with its vocabulary, rhythm and flow.

3 Using a quality dictionary, look up the meaning of any words you are unsure of. Annotate these definitions. A dictionary often gives several meanings for a word so you need to pick the meaning that fits the poem.

**Look for:**

4 the subject

5 the poet's attitude towards the subject, often revealed as 'tone'

6 the theme.

**Then look for:**

7 images, perhaps created by use of figures of speech

8 effective words (diction, vocabulary)

9 patterns like sentence structure, verses, rhyme.

**Then ask yourself:**

10 what do I think about the poem and its ideas?


ISBN 9780170233293

## Terminology you should be confident with …

You are in your final year of studying poetry at school and by now it is important to include the technical language of English in your answer. The list below is what we would expect you to know at this level.

You will notice in the left hand margin there are two circles labelled 'I know' and 'I need to check'. Read through the list and tick the box that best describes your knowledge of each literary term. Look up all the ones you don't know in the Language Lists at the end of this book.

| I know | I need to check | | I know | I need to check | | I know | I need to check | |
|---|---|---|---|---|---|---|---|---|
| ○ | ○ | Alliteration | ○ | ○ | Extended metaphor | ○ | ○ | Rhyme |
| ○ | ○ | Antithesis | ○ | ○ | Imagery | ○ | ○ | Rhythm |
| ○ | ○ | Apostrophe | ○ | ○ | Metaphor | ○ | ○ | Sibilance |
| ○ | ○ | Assonance | ○ | ○ | Onomatopoeia | ○ | ○ | Simile |
| ○ | ○ | Caesura | ○ | ○ | Oxymoron | ○ | ○ | Symbolism |
| ○ | ○ | End-stopped line | ○ | ○ | Personification | | | |
| ○ | ○ | Enjambment | ○ | ○ | Repetition | | | |

**We thought we would remind you about:**

### Punctuating Poetry

#### Caesura

A natural pause or a break in a line of poetry, usually indicated by a punctuation mark.

For example: When will the bell ring, and end this weariness?

*(D.H. Lawrence, Last Lesson of the Afternoon)*

#### Enjambment

When the meaning of a line of poetry is completed on the next line.

For example: How long have they tugged the leash, and strained apart,
My pack of unruly hounds. *(D.H. Lawrence, Last Lesson of the Afternoon)*

This technique can emphasise an idea or add to the rhythm and flow of the lines.

#### End-stopped line

The lines of a stanza that have a grammatical pause at the end of each line.

For example: I can haul and urge them no more. *(D.H. Lawrence, Last Lesson of the Afternoon)*

This technique completes an idea visually and grammatically.

**Why?** Because if you read the poem to the punctuation then understanding the poem is so much easier.

ISBN 9780170233293

## The language of poetry

To sum up, this chart draws together all of the terminology you will use as you close read poetry. Use it as a reference whenever you look at an unfamiliar poem.

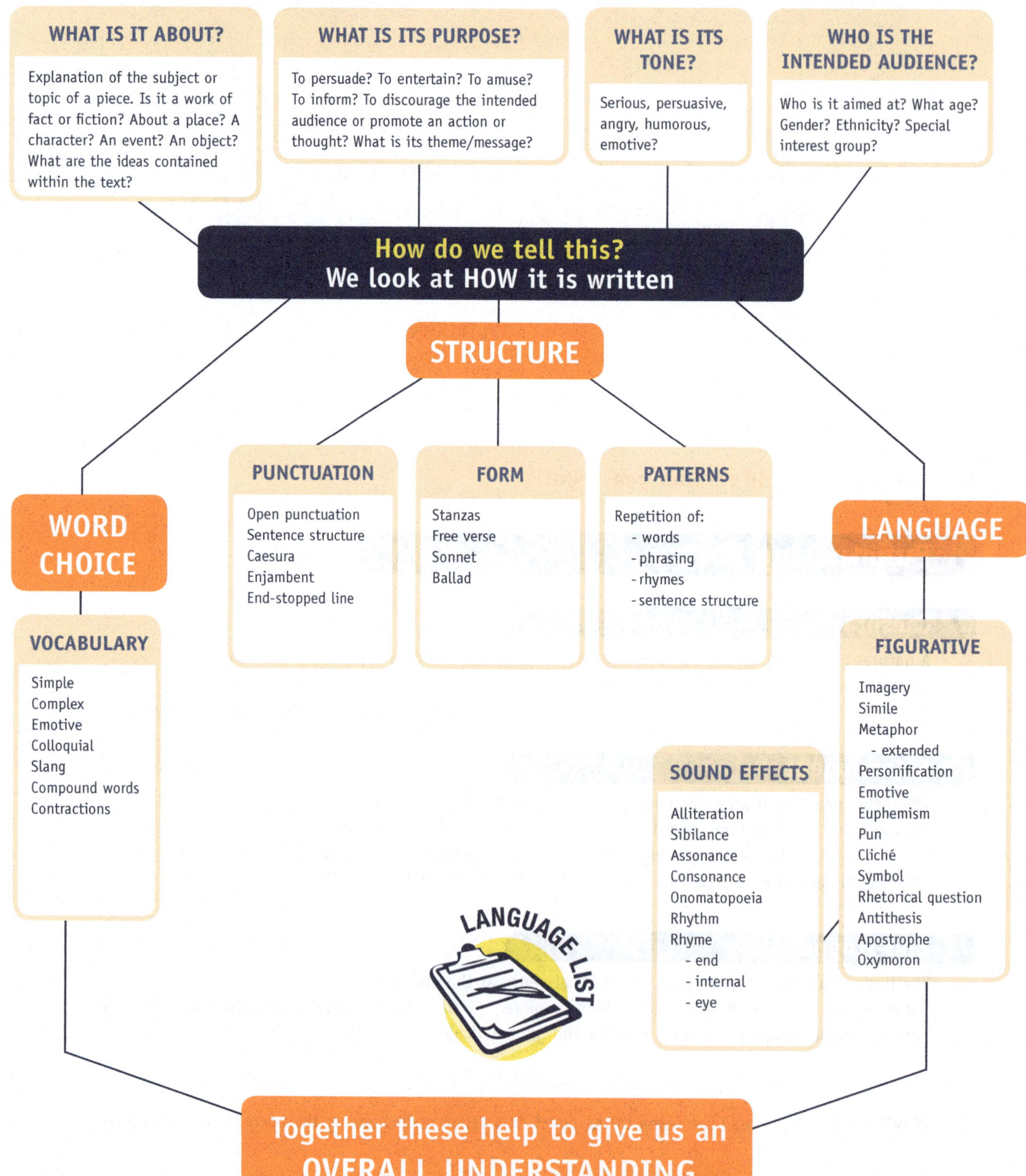




ISBN 9780170233293

## Let's look at a poem together

This poem, written by Vernon Scannell, is concerned with a childhood experience. Use the same approach as you did for the prose passages. Poetry and prose use words in much the same ways. However, it is important to read poetry to the punctuation, not to the lines. Read it aloud, if possible – it helps with understanding.

Read the poem carefully several times. As you do so, highlight the end rhymes. Notice the punctuation. Highlight and annotate examples of repetition, simile, metaphor, onomatopoeia and any other language features you notice. See how many words are more than a single syllable.

We have given you some straightforward questions to answer briefly as annotated notes, which will assist you to understand the poem fully. These annotations should help you to form a complete detailed answer to the final question.

### A Case of Murder

They should not have left him there alone,
Alone that is except for the cat.
He was only nine, not old enough
To be left alone in a basement flat,
Alone, that is, except for the cat.
A dog would have been a different thing,
A big gruff dog with slashing jaws,
But a cat with round eyes mad as gold,
Plump as a cushion with tucked-in paws---
Better have left him with a fair-sized rat!
But what they did was leave him with a cat.
He hated that cat; he watched it sit,
A buzzing machine of soft black stuff,
He sat and watched and he hated it,
Snug in its fur, hot blood in a muff,
And its mad gold stare and the way it sat
Crooning dark warmth: he loathed all that.

1 Who is 'they'?

2 How old is the child?

3 Description of cat's eyes suggests what?

4 What does he hate about the cat?

ISBN 9780170233293

So he took Daddy's stick and he hit the cat.
Then quick as a sudden crack in glass
It hissed, black flash, to a hiding place
In the dust and dark beneath the couch,
And he followed the grin on his new-made face,
A wide-eyed, frightened snarl of a grin,
And he took the stick and he thrust it in,
Hard and quick in the furry dark.
The black fur squealed and he felt his skin
Prickle with sparks of dry delight.
Then the cat again came into sight,
Shot for the door that wasn't quite shut,
But the boy, quick too, slammed fast the door:
The cat, half-through, was cracked like a nut
And the soft black thud was dumped on the floor.
Then the boy was suddenly terrified
And he bit his knuckles and cried and cried;
But he had to do something with the dead thing there.
His eyes squeezed beads of salty prayer
But the wound of fear gaped wide and raw;
He dared not touch the thing with his hands
So he fetched a spade and shovelled it
And dumped the load of heavy fur
In the spidery cupboard under the stair
Where it's been for years, and though it died
It's grown in that cupboard and its hot low purr
Grows slowly louder year by year:
There'll not be a corner for the boy to hide
When the cupboard swells and all sides split
And the huge black cat pads out of it.

*Vernon Scannell*

5 Why is Daddy's stick relevant?

6 Why does the boy grin?

7 What effect do the rhymes, the single syllable words and onomatopeia have on this poem?

8 Why does he cry?

9 Why does the purr grow louder?

10 What does the huge black cat symbolise?


ISBN 9780170233293

**Answer the following question in as much detail as possible. Use quotations and references to the text to support your ideas.**

What is the poet saying about childhood experiences in this poem?

Remember your annotations will help you scaffold an answer with depth and detail ...

ISBN 9780170233293

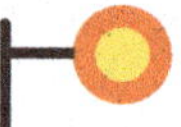

# Poetry close reading practice

A variety of poetic text and accompanying questions are provided in this section to help you practise answering close reading questions.

## Text 1

Read the following poem. Look up words you don't know the meaning of and annotate important features (see pages 155-163).

### An Arundel Tomb

I Side by side, their faces blurred,
The earl and countess lie in stone,
Their proper habits vaguely shown
As jointed armour, stiffened pleat,
And that faint hint of the absurd—
The little dogs under their feet.

II Such plainness of the pre-baroque
Hardly involves the eye, until
It meets his left-hand gauntlet, still
Clasped empty in the other; and
One sees, with a sharp tender shock,
His hand withdrawn, holding her hand.

III They would not think to lie so long.
Such faithfulness in effigy
Was just a detail friends would see:
A sculptor's sweet commissioned grace
Thrown off in helping to prolong
The Latin names around the base.

IV They would not guess how early in
Their supine stationary voyage
The air would change to soundless damage,
Turn the old tenantry away;
How soon succeeding eyes begin
To look, not read. Rigidly they

V Persisted, linked through lengths and breadths
Of time. Snow fell, undated. Light
Each summer thronged the glass. A bright
Litter of birdcalls strewed the same



ISBN 9780170233293

Bone-riddled ground. And up the paths
The endless altered people came,
VI Washing at their identity.
Now, helpless in the hollow of
An unarmorial age, a trough
Of smoke in slow suspended skeins
Above their scrap of history,
Only an attitude remains:
VII Time has transfigured them into
Untruth. The stone fidelity
They hardly meant has come to be
Their final blazon, and to prove
Our almost-instinct almost true:
What will survive of us is love.

*Philip Larkin*

## An aside on ... rhyme

We use the alphabet to represent rhyme patterns. Using a letter to represent the sound of the last syllable in each line, you can see that this poem follows a regular rhyme pattern abbcac – the same for each verse.

It is very difficult to write well in this way. Try it!

## An aside on ... rhythm

This is the system used to look at poetry that is written in a formal rhyme and rhythm pattern. A line can be divided into 'feet' each containing one accented syllable with one or more unaccented syllables attached to it. If the pattern is two syllables with the stress on the second, this is called an iambic rhythm. This poem uses iambic rhythm.

˘ / ˘ / ˘ / ˘ /
The earl/ and coun/tess lie/ in stone

This rhythm is the closest to natural speech patterns in English. You will see it in the Shakespeare you are studying, too.

ISBN 9780170233293

**Answer the following questions in as much detail as possible. Use quotations and references to the text to support your ideas.**

1 **Verses I and II**

Describe the tomb that the poet is writing about. Why is it different from the usual ones? How does the poet draw our attention to the difference?

2 **Verse III**

Comment on the structure of the first line and the effect created by it. What does the poet suggest about the sculpture in the rest of this verse?

3 **Verse IV**

What is the overall meaning of this verse? Comment on the examples the poet uses.

4 **Verse V**

Identify and comment on the series of images used in this verse.



ISBN 9780170233293

5 **Verse VI**

What is the mood of this verse? How does the poet's choice of words create this mood?

6 **Verse VII**

In your own words, explain the poet's final decision about the tomb as revealed in this verse and its message to us. Do you agree with him?

ISBN 9780170233293

## Text 2

Read the following poem. Look up words you don't know the meaning of and annotate important features (see pages 155-163).

### Metaphors

I'm a riddle in nine syllables,
An elephant, a ponderous house,
A melon strolling on two tendrils.
O red fruit, ivory, fine timbers!
This loaf's big with its yeasty rising.
Money's new-minted in this fat purse.
I'm a means, a stage, a cow in calf.
I've eaten a bag of green apples,
Boarded the train there's no getting off.

*Sylvia Plath*

### First ...

On the lines provided below explain in your own words what each metaphor refers to.

Think about:

- how the first line is reflected in the poem's imagery and structure.
- what the final line means.
- how the poet feels about the condition she is in.

1 ______________________________

2 ______________________________

3 ______________________________

4 ______________________________

5 ______________________________

6 ______________________________

7 ______________________________

8 ______________________________

9 ______________________________


ISBN 9780170233293

**Answer the following question in as much detail as possible. Use quotations and references to the text to support your ideas.**

Explain the way the poem has been structured, its meaning and how the poet is feeling about herself. (Be sure to complete all three parts of this response.)

ISBN 9780170233293

## Text 3

Read the following poem. Look up words you don't know the meaning of and annotate important features (see pages 155-163).

'In Tenebris' means 'In Darkness'. The poem has a Latin epigraph (brief inscription or quotation usually on a coin, statue etc) from *Psalm 102*, which is written in English in the King James version of the Bible as 'My heart is smitten, and withered like grass'.

### In Tenebris

*'Percussus sum sicut foenum, et aruit cor meum.'*

Wintertime nighs;
But my bereavement-pain
It cannot bring again:
Twice no one dies.
Flower-petals flee;
But, since it once hath been,
No more that severing scene
Can harrow me.
Birds faint in dread:
I shall not lose old strength
In the lone frost's black length:
Strength long since fled!
Leaves freeze to dun;
But friends can not turn cold
This season as of old
For him with none.
Tempests may scath;
But love can not make smart
Again this year his heart
Who no heart hath.
Black is night's cope;
But death will not appal
One who, past doubtings all,
Waits in unhope.

*Thomas Hardy (1840–1928)*



ISBN 9780170233293

**Answer the following questions in as much detail as possible. Use quotations and references to the text to support your ideas.**

1 How do the poem's title and epigraph prepare you for the content of the poem?

2 Comment on the way the structure of the poem contributes to its meaning.

3 Choose two of these poetic techniques used by the poet: metaphor, coinage, pronouns, imagery. Give example/s and describe the effect of each one you choose.

i

ii

4 Comment on the word order of the last line of the poem.

5 What is the tone of the poem? Support your answer with reference to the poem.

ISBN 9780170233293

## Text 4

Read the following poem. Look up words you don't know the meaning of and annotate important features (see pages 155-163).

### Death of a Naturalist

All year the flax-dam festered in the heart
Of the townland; green and heavy headed
Flax had rotted there, weighted down by huge sods.
Daily it sweltered in the punishing sun.
Bubbles gargled delicately, bluebottles
Wove a strong gauze of sound around the smell.
There were dragon-flies, spotted butterflies,
But best of all was the warm thick slobber
Of frogspawn that grew like clotted water
In the shade of the banks. Here, every spring
I would fill jampotfuls of the jellied
Specks to range on window-sills at home,
On shelves at school, and wait and watch until
The fattening dots burst into nimble-
Swimming tadpoles. Miss Walls would tell us how
The daddy frog was called a bullfrog
And how he croaked and how the mammy frog
Laid hundreds of little eggs and this was
Frogspawn. You could tell the weather by frogs too
For they were yellow in the sun and brown
In rain.
Then one hot day when fields were rank
With cowdung in the grass the angry frogs
Invaded the flax-dam; I ducked through hedges
To a coarse croaking that I had not heard
Before. The air was thick with a bass chorus.
Right down the dam gross-bellied frogs were cocked
On sods; their loose necks pulsed like sails. Some hopped:
The slap and plop were obscene threats. Some sat
Poised like mud grenades, their blunt heads farting.
I sickened, turned, and ran. The great slime kings
Were gathered there for vengeance and I knew
That if I dipped my hand the spawn would clutch it.

*Seamus Heaney*



ISBN 9780170233293

### First …

The poem divides naturally into two sections.

Annotate the first section with notes on when and where the event takes place. Look for words that tell you how old the narrator is. Is there any effective imagery, onomatopoeia, similes; any special vocabulary?

Now turn to the second part of the poem. What has happened? What is the dominant image and which words reinforce it? Highlight them. Why does the child think the frogs gathered for vengeance? What does the poem's title add to this part of the narrative? Annotate the poem with your ideas.

**When you think you understand the meaning of the poem, answer the following questions in as much detail as possible. Use quotations and references to the text to support your ideas.**

1 Is the title comic or serious? Give your reasons.

2 Comment on how the child learns at school and home about frogs.

3 How does the child's imagination make him see the plague of frogs? What does he do?

4 Choose at least one example of onomatopoeia in the poem and explain why the poet has used it.

5 What general comment do you think this poem is making about childhood?

ISBN 9780170233293

## Text 5

Read the following poem. Look up words you don't know the meaning of and annotate important features (see pages 155-163).

### My parents dancing

We, in our fancy dress, were feasting
at long trestles covered in white paper
soon stained by gobs of raspberry jelly
and wet by icecream and icecream spoons.

We had danced in a lightly-controlled fashion
cowboys and fairies, each with their passion
and holding hands passed down along avenues
of garland space and returned to captivity.

Our little energies increased our identities.
Finally, in the Grand Parade, we made a globe
our colours smudged, we ran to eat
at trestle tables, treats piled up.

But on the vacant, vaster floor
more like sea, more like a shore
my parents among the other parents dance
and I cannot forbear to glance

at how they glide and corner and dip
as if, loosing their children, they resume
the leading reins that held between
their forms and passion that adored

and which they leave a space for
as if they too treasure it, leaning away
then irresistibly drawn into its pull
and yet drawing slightly back to accord

it homage. It might be the space
between their twin pillows at night
or a hand's reach behind a head
or her hair that lightly touches his shoulder.

*Elizabeth Smither*


ISBN 9780170233293

### First …

Read the poem carefully and notice …

- the subject and style divide between verses 3 and 4
- alliteration
- similes
- metaphor
- words suggesting movement.

**When you think you understand the meaning of the poem, answer the following questions in as much detail as possible. Use quotations and references to the text to support your ideas.**

1 What is happening in verses 1–3?

2 How does the writer's change of style in verse 4 reflect the ideas in the poem?

3 Comment on the change in focus in lines 13–14

4 What does the child notice about her parents as they dance?

ISBN 9780170233293

## Text 6

Read the following poem. Look up words you don't know the meaning of and annotate important features (see pages 155-163).

### You're Telling Me

Those boring, corny stories
you'll see
they're the ones'll make you weep.

Now when your folks do their reruns,
the Olds' slow same-olds,
their yeah, you've told mes,
you scrape your chair back from the table
that little bit too quickly,
do a cover-up by clearing plates
(you just can't stand that wet look on their faces)
be excused, go to your room,
make your cassette deck dial climb up past that notch
your dad marked off in indelible pen,
rebel in decibels, against—what?
The same-old, whatever they've got.

But you'll cotton on.
Find memory's hereditary,
with its cataleptic seizures
in the middle of the nowhere of your life—
times when you turn to whoever's there to say
did I tell you that one about the night
when my dad just made like a beeline,
jumped dozens of fences for her
to poach hundreds of daffodils
yellow as yolks done in butter,
or how once, in front of everyone,
he sprinted up the down escalator
just to be with her a few minutes sooner?
Or, you'll say, as whoever's gaze it is slips away
the one about how I never did tell him
I'd listened?

*Emma Neale*


ISBN 9780170233293

### First …

Read the poem carefully and notice …

- colloquial words
- slang
- clichés
- short lines
- metaphor
- similes
- verse structure.

**Answer the following questions in as much detail as possible. Use quotations and references to the text to support your ideas.**

1 In verse 2 what is the poet saying about the way teenagers react to their parents' reminiscences?

2 In verse 3 how does she suggest this will change?

3 Summarise the kinds of things she says children will remember. Is she adding her personal memories? How can you tell?

ISBN 9780170233293

4 Comment on the way the structure of the first and last verses contributes to their meaning.

Think about:

- length of lines
- use of cliché
- change of pronoun.



ISBN 9780170233293

# Making connections: texts 5 and 6

It is not unusual to be asked to make comparisons, or to draw connections, between two texts. These two poems do have similarities. We look at the comparison question on page 87. You might like to read this page before you answer this question.

**Now that you have analysed texts 5 and 6 answer the following question in as much detail as possible. Use quotations and references to the texts to support your ideas.**

Examine the similarities and the differences between Elizabeth Smither's *My Parents Dancing* and Emma Neale's *You're Telling Me*.

ISBN 9780170233293

# An aside on ... visual text

The *Achievement English* series has never been designed solely for assessment. We are aiming to develop your understanding of, and ability to respond to, everything you read, see or hear. Think about it. Every day you read news or blogs on the Internet; you hear opinion and lyrics on the radio; you browse through a magazine; you read a novel or a non-fiction book. Plus every other classroom you go into, with its posters and its text books, presents you with words and images to think about.

Close reading is not restricted to assessment in English classes.

It is a universal skill.

You have spent a lot of this book concentrating on analysing written text – whether that would be poetry or prose. We thought we would give you a chance to test what you have learnt on a visual text.

## Have a go ...

See how many of the following language techniques you can highlight on the text of the following advertisement. Use the Visual Language List on page 155-163 if you need to remind yourself of some of these terms.

- Analogy
- Adjective
- Compound word/neologism
- Effective vocabulary
- Humour
- Hyperbole
- Imperative
- Juxtaposition
- Onomatopoeia
- Personal pronoun
- Pun



ISBN 9780170233293

## Killinchy Gold

Look carefully at the visual text below and answer the following questions in as much detail as possible.

ISBN 9780170233293

**Now you have identified the language techniques see if you can answer the following questions:**

1 How has the audience's attention been caught by the headline?

FOR GREAT ICE CREAM OUR FOREFATHERS ENDURED SUFFERING, DEPRIVATION, AND THE EVER-PRESENT THREAT OF BRAINFREEZE.

2 How do the visual elements of the advertisement come together to support the idea of Killinchy Gold ice cream originating in the 19th century?

3 Clearly explain, with detail from the text, the connection between the verbal and visual elements of this advertisement.



ISBN 9780170233293

4 Explain the connection of the last paragraph to the rest of the advertisement.

5 Part of the effectiveness of this advertisement comes from the tone of the body copy. Comment on the style of the writing and how it has been achieved.

**NCEA assessments will separate the close reading of unfamiliar written text (AS 3.3) and visual and oral text (AS 3.9).**

ISBN 9780170233293

7

# Compare ... Contrast ... Connect

By now you have been asked to look for connections between texts on more than one occasion.

These three words: compare, contrast and connect, sit at the heart of this type of question.

So let's think about what might be similar, what might connect texts:

| COMPARE | CONTRAST | CONNECT |
|---|---|---|
| Emphasise **similarities** and mention differences. | Compare by showing **differences.** | **Link together** related elements. |

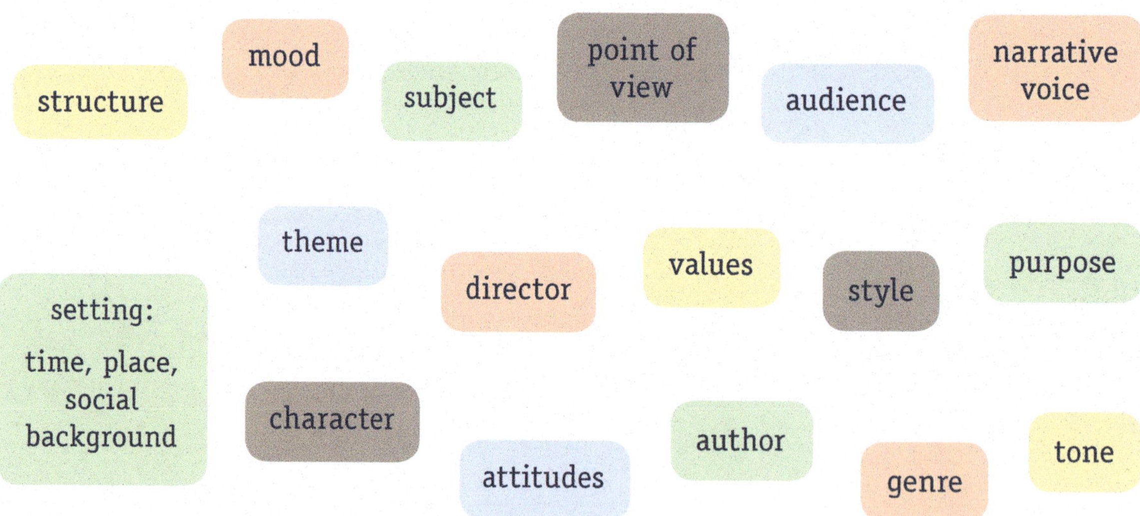


These are not new words, are they? We repeat, you will be using the same ways to analyse these texts as all the others you have studied in the past; it's just that the focus will be different.



ISBN 9780170233293

# The comparison question

It is possible that you will be asked to **compare** and **contrast** two pieces of writing. These two words have specific meanings:

**Compare:** observe the similarity or relation between two things.

**Contrast:** set two things in opposition, so as to show their differences.

This means that you are looking for **similarities** and **differences** between the two pieces.

One way to tackle such a question is to draw up a simple table to help you plan your response.

- In classroom practice this can be completed slowly and carefully to provide the details for your response.
- In an assessment it can be a quick jotting down of ideas to give an overall structure to your response.

First of all ask yourself some straightforward questions about the two pieces. You might annotate the pieces with notes indicating what you have noticed.

### Start with WHAT?

Do they have a narrator or are they written in the 3rd person?

Is the narrator the writer? If not, who is the narrator?

Are the pieces fiction, non-fiction, poetry, prose?

What is the subject of the pieces?

Do they share a mood/tone/atmosphere?

### Then WHEN? and WHERE?

Modern, historical? Morning, evening? New Zealand, overseas? Rural, urban?

### Then try WHY?

Do they have a similar theme?

Is there a message that they share?

### And then HOW?

Consider the use of techniques like:

- voice
- tense
- syntax, punctuation
- figures of speech – e.g. metaphor, simile, alliteration, assonance
- symbolism, imagery
- structure, shape, rhyme, rhythm

Then construct a table like this to help you use what you have noticed.

| Similarities | Text One e.g. | Text Two e.g. |
|---|---|---|
| | | |
| | | |
| | | |
| | | |

| Differences | Text One e.g. | Text Two e.g. |
|---|---|---|
| | | |
| | | |
| | | |
| | | |

ISBN 9780170233293

## Let's compare and contrast two poems ...

Read the following poems. Look up words you don't know the meaning of and annotate important features (see pages 155-163).

### My Love Is Like To Ice

My love is like to ice, and I to fire:
How comes it then that this her cold so great
Is not dissolved through my so hot desire,
But harder grows the more I her entreat?
Or how comes it that my exceeding heat
Is not allayed by her heart-frozen cold,
But that I burn much more in boiling sweat,
And feel my flames augmented manifold?
What more miraculous thing may be told,
That fire, which all things melts, should harden ice,
And ice, which is congeal'd with senseless cold,
Should kindle fire by wonderful device?
Such is the power of love in gentle mind,
That it can alter all the course of kind.

*Edmund Spenser (1552-1599)*



ISBN 9780170233293

## Fire and Ice

Some say the world will end in fire,
Some say in ice.
From what I've tasted of desire
I hold with those who favor fire.
But if it had to perish twice,
I think I know enough of hate
To know that for destruction ice
Is also great
And would suffice.

*Robert Frost (1874-1963)*
*(publ. 1920)*

We suggest that you might like to investigate the ideas found in Canto 32 of Dante's *Inferno* and what Aristotle has to say about sins of reason and sins of passion to help you with Robert Frost's 'Fire and Ice'. Understanding the convention known as 'Courtly Love' popular in the 16th century will help you appreciate Spenser's sonnet, 'My love is like to ice…', as will knowing something of the conventions surrounding the sonnet form itself. Use the Internet or books of criticism in your school's library to help you approach these works with confidence.

And a final reminder – always use a dictionary to find the meanings of words you do not understand. Every word in a poem is carefully chosen by the poet and deserves your effort to understand the meaning fully.

ISBN 9780170233293

**Fill in more of these tables from what you have noticed about the poems.**

| Similarities | My love is like to ice | Fire and Ice |
|---|---|---|
| Use of personal pronoun – first person | My love is like … | I hold with those … |
| Uses regular rhythm | iambic<br>e.g. | iambic<br>e.g. |
| | | |
| | | |

| Differences | My love is like to ice | Fire and Ice |
|---|---|---|
| Subject matter | Is about a personal experience | Is about humanity as a whole |
| Tone | Casual, sounds like conversation, deceptively understated | Formal, lots of rhetorical questions |
| | | |
| | | |



ISBN 9780170233293

**Armed with this information you should be able to compose a strong response to the compare and contrast question.**

Compare and contrast these two poems, focusing your answer on the way the poets have chosen to use the idea of fire and the idea of ice.

Note: Examination questions tend to ask for 400 words. It is useful to extend this limit in situations where you are not working to time.

ISBN 9780170233293

**Here is a possible response:**

These two poems use the concept of fire and ice to symbolise feelings. In Frost's 'Fire and Ice', the poet begins with a simple statement 'Some say the world will end in fire,/ Some say in ice.' He seems to be writing about a possible scientific end to our world – through conflagration or a new ice age. However, as the poem progresses it is clear that he is using the word 'fire to symbolise passion – 'From what I've tasted of desire/ I hold with those who favor fire' and 'ice' to symbolise hatred – '... I know enough of hate/ To know that for destruction ice/ Is also great ...'

In Spenser's sonnet, he tells us that the woman he loves passionately rejects his affection '... this her cold so great/ Is not dissolved through my so hot desire.' The poem goes on to generalise about how the inability of their human nature to change each other's feelings is the opposite of nature itself where heat tempers cold and vice versa.

Frost's poem is written in the first person and in a casual, almost laconic style that sounds just like conversation but it is in fact carefully structured into iambic 8 or 4 feet lines. The shorter lines focus on the syllable 'ice' and with the repetition of this syllable '... ice ... twice ... suffice ... ice' he draws attention to the negative connotation of hate that he tells us is able to destroy us all. This is a huge idea but presented as if it were a casual comment.

Spenser, on the other hand, gives a simple human emotion huge significance. Writing 400 years ago and following the sonnet's 14 line iambic pentameter structure, he writes in rhetorical questions, pointing out how heat and cold – passion and dislike – are not behaving in the human heart as they do in nature. He completes the poem with a concluding couplet expressing amazement over the power of love, which makes the poem feel positive though it really is expressing a sadness.

Both poets have used the concept of fire and ice as symbolising passion and hatred but have applied the idea differently – one to human behaviour as a group, the other as individuals.


ISBN 9780170233293

# Let's have a look at a poem and a newspaper article together

**Background:**

Rameses II was King of Egypt in the 1200s BC.

Over 3000 years later, in the early 19th century, the poet Percy Bysshe Shelley wrote a poem called *Ozymandias* (the Greek name for Rameses) in which he purports to present a traveller's experience of seeing a broken statue in a desert.

200 years later journalist Cahal Milmo, writing for a British daily newspaper, chose to use a quotation from the poem to begin an article on the collapse of Saddam Hussein's regime in Iraq.

**Read both the poem and the article carefully. Answer the following questions in as much detail as possible. Use quotations and references to the text to support your ideas.**

## Ozymandias

I met a traveller from an antique land
Who said:—Two vast and trunkless legs of stone
Stand in the desert. Near them on the sand,
Half sunk, a shatter'd visage lies, whose frown
And wrinkled lip and sneer of cold command
Tell that its sculptor well those passions read
Which yet survive, stamp'd on these lifeless things,
The hand that mock'd them and the heart that fed.
And on the pedestal these words appear:
"My name is Ozymandias, king of kings:
Look on my works, ye mighty, and despair!"
Nothing beside remains: round the decay
Of that colossal wreck, boundless and bare,
The lone and level sands stretch far away.

*Percy Bysshe Shelley*

ISBN 9780170233293

# Residence fit for a king of kings

## RAID: US soldiers settle into fake baroque furniture and shower among the gold

By Cahal Milmo

*"My name is Ozymandias, king of kings: Look on my works, ye mighty, and despair!" Nothing beside remains: round the decay, Of that colossal wreck, boundless and bare, The lone and level sands stretch far away.*

They are the echoing monuments to Iraq's own crumbling pharaoh. Built on the proceeds of his country's oil wealth while his people relied on UN handouts, the doors of some of Saddam Hussein's palaces were thrown open yesterday in the chaos of the war to unseat him.

Shortly after 6am, a phalanx of American soldiers burst through the carved mahogany entrance to the New Presidential Palace in central Baghdad, with its sweeping views of the Tigris and hectares of marble flooring. Until four weeks ago, the inner circle of President Saddam's regime may well have sat here discussing their next move to stave off an invasion across the desert wastes.

Last night, a group of grimy GIs was installed amid the gilt furnishings of the Iraqi President in preparation for the takeover of his capital. One soldier suggested he would be having his "first shower in weeks" in the remains of one of the bathrooms where water was still running. In a nearby room, US Army Staff Sergeant Chad Touchett sat back in a faux antique drawing room chair drawing deeply on a cigarette, surrounded by five compadres from Company A.

The palace had not even been defended by the special Republican Guard, the elite force handed the task of guarding the Iraqi leader's "inner cordon". Instead, a confused group of Syrian mercenaries had given it up with minimal resistance – one was hiding in the walk-in fridge – when confronted by the force of 70 American tanks and 60 armoured personnel carriers.

Underlining the sense among the members of the US 3rd Infantry Regiment that their occupation of the enemy's lair was a symbolic victory, Captain Chris Carter, of Watkinsville, Georgia, said: "I do believe this city is freakin' ours."

Their arrival demonstrated that not only was the Iraqi leader's power rapidly waning but also its trappings – ostentatiously amassed at an estimated cost of $4.3bn in the past 12 years alone and as outrageous in their boundless ambition as the man who commissioned them – were liable for summary confiscation by the US government.

President Saddam, like Shelley's Ozymandias, the supreme ruler of ancient Egypt – as Rameses II – likes to crown his victories with the construction of monolithic edifices to stare out over the battlefield.

And some three millennia after Rameses II, Iraq's King of Kings has busied himself since his "triumph" in the 1991 Gulf War – building at least 48 People's Palaces, forbidden to his people by guns and 30ft walls.

The New Presidential Palace, a confection of sand-coloured brick topped with a glittering blue-and-gold dome of ceramic tiles, was completed last year to stand close to the headquarters of the pillar of President Saddam's Iraq, the Baath Party.

As Colin Brazier, of Sky News, one of the reporters accompanying the US forces, put it: "It's an extraordinarily decadent structure. There is Italian marble and gold gilt everywhere. It's about as opulent as you could possibly imagine."

Of the original four floors of the palace, only two were left intact after repeated targeting by American and British aircraft. Parts of the remaining first floor and basement were awash with flood water. But inside, the accoutrements of a regime hooked on glitz and grandeur remained intact: imitation French baroque furniture covered in dust, several televisions in each room, a rooftop swimming pool and, of course, the decor essential for every maniacal despot from Hitler to Nicolae Ceausescu, a marble bathroom with 24-carat gold taps. And, outside is a symbol of the American good life – President Saddam's barbecue.

### >> Saddam's palaces

- > The total area covered by President Saddam's palaces is some 30.5 sq km a third of which is covered in artificial lakes, which the Iraqi leader likes to fish.
- > At least 48 of the structures have been built since the end of the 1991 Gulf War at a cost of $4.3bn.
- > They were monuments to a mighty tyrant. Now Saddam's palaces symbolise a crumbling regime.

For the US soldiers leading the incursion into the heart of Baghdad, it was an opportunity to perform the rite of war that accompanies the final days of an autocrat grown fat while his people dwindle – the vicarious thrill of rifling through a dictator's intimate possessions.

The troops leafed through documents and thick vellum stationery, before helping themselves to a few souvenirs in the form of ashtrays, duck-down pillows and gold-painted glassware. It was the equivalent of turning out Imelda Marcos's shoeboxes or rummaging under Idi Amin's bed.

Here was a monument to President Saddam's wastefulness. Beyond the bulkier furnishings and a few plates and dishes in the kitchen, the palace had been cleared of most of its contents. And in true nouveau-riche style, from one gilded and mother-of-pearl soap dish hangs the label attesting that it came from a plush Western supplier. Carrying the manufacturer's initials PD, it read: "Gold-plate finish, pure 24-carat gold."

The total area covered by President Saddam's palaces is some 30.5 sq km – a third of which is covered in artificial lakes, which the Iraqi leader likes to fish. At least 48 of the structures have been built since the end of the 1991 Gulf War at a cost of $4.3bn. According to the Americans, the money was siphoned from the proceeds of oil smuggling and the resale of World Food Programme rations.

The palaces are not only homes but military strongholds of the man who considers himself a latter-day Saladin, vanquisher of the Crusader armies and leader of all the Muslims. The jewel is the Republican Palace in Baghdad, which consists of more than 700 buildings including President Saddam's private offices, the headquarters of the Special Security Force and a bunker designed to withstand nuclear attack.

—The Independent (UK), 08 April 2003



ISBN 9780170233293

**Answer the following questions in as much detail as possible. Use quotations and references to the text to support your ideas.**

1 In the poem Shelley suggests the kind of ruler Ozymandias was. Describe him and then give examples from the newspaper article that suggest Saddam Hussein was a similar kind of ruler.

2 How does the journalist suggest that Saddam Hussein was not a rational person?

3 In the article how does the journalist contrast the US troops and those other soldiers fighting in Iraq?

ISBN 9780170233293

4 Choose three of the underlined words or phrases in the article and explain the meaning and effect of each one.

| | | |
|---|---|---|
| *phalanx* | *hooked on glitz* | *faux antique* |
| *hectares of marble flooring* | *"triumph"* | *confection* |
| *freakin'* | *autocrat* | |

5 In the poem, Shelley quotes the words written at the base of the statue. Explain in your own words the irony in the meaning of these words.

6 This article might be said to be biased or written from a particular standpoint. Why might this be? How can you tell?



ISBN 9780170233293

Below you will find an example of how another Year 13 student tackled this work. The student's answers have been marked and there are marker's comments. Mark your own answers from the guidelines.

1 In the poem Shelley suggests the kind of ruler Ozymandias was. Describe the kind of ruler Ozymandias seems to be in the poem, and then give examples from the newspaper article that suggest Saddam Hussein was a similar kind of ruler.

Ozymandias is described as being an extravagant, defiant, arrogant ruler. Saddam is also extravagant – building 48 palaces in 12 years, defiantly reselling aid packages and arrogantly thinking of the Gulf War as victory.

This answer is far too brief and superficial. Although the student has understood the essentials and produced three useful adjectives to describe Ozymandias, he or she has failed to show his or her pathway to understanding by giving evidence from the texts. You must use examples from the poem and passage to support any points you make. The answer might also draw a conclusion, linking the two parts of the answer together.

The response could be improved thus:

Ozymandias is described in the poem as being an arrogant ruler – his statue quotes him as calling himself 'King of Kings'. He was extravagant, having a 'vast' statue built to himself and was a harsh ruler with his 'sneer of cold command'. The article suggests that Hussein is similar. His arrogance is illustrated by Milmo's reference to the way he 'liked to crown his victories with the construction of monolithic edifices to stare out over the battlefield'. He, too, is extravagant: spending $4.3 billion on 48 'opulent' palaces since 1991 and he was a harsh ruler, building these palaces 'on the proceeds of his country's oil wealth while his people relied on United Nations handouts'. The journalist has used the quotation from the poem to point out that dictators through the centuries show similar traits and patterns of behaviour.

2 How does the journalist suggest that Saddam Hussein was not a rational person?

The journalist suggests that Saddam Hussein was not a rational person by the descriptions of his palaces 'ostentatiously amassed at an estimated cost of $4.3 billion in the past 12 years alone and as outrageous in their boundless ambition

ISBN 9780170233293

as the man who commissioned them'. He built so-called Peoples Palaces that were in reality 'forbidden to his people by guns and 9m walls'.

The best part of this answer is the phrase 'so-called'. Here the student is offering a comment on the irony of the naming of these palaces as for the people when they were so clearly not.

There are other parts of the article that might have offered examples to improve the level of the response. Milmo compares Hussein's taste in decor to that of Hitler and Nicolae Ceaucescu, both accepted 'maniacal despots' and his possessions to those of Imelda Marcos and Idi Amin, also former leaders of nations, now in disrepute. He also implies that the palaces were follies – including the 700-room 'monument to Saddam's wastefulness', as he could not possibly use them all.

3 In the article how does the journalist contrast the US troops and those other soldiers fighting in Iraq?

The journalist says that rather than having the Special Republican Guard guarding the palace, there was a group of confused Syrian mercenaries, who gave up the palace rather easily. The Americans are much more organised than the other troops that Saddam has put in place. The US soldiers come in as a 'phalanx', the other troops were a 'group'.

In this answer the student begins to answer the question in the final sentence, although they do not explain why the two words have such differing connotations.

The key words in the question are **how** and **contrast.** An excellent answer will use the examples found to construct an integrated response that reaches a conclusion. It might well include material like this:

Words used to describe the Americans include the nouns 'soldiers', 'troops', 'phalanx', which suggest a structured, well-organised unit. The nouns 'comrades' and 'compadres', suggest they are organised and working together for a common purpose. The opposition they meet is 'a confused group' of Syrian mercenaries, people who fight for money and who, the words suggest, have no leadership, organisation or common purpose. The passage also names several American soldiers and draws attention to their rank and the US equipment: tanks and armoured personnel carriers. They 'burst' into the Palace and sit and smoke comfortably after the attack. In contrast, the Iraqi Special Republican Guard is not 'even' there, the mercenaries put up 'minimal resistance' and no mention is


ISBN 9780170233293

made of their weapons. The only Syrian to be singled out is the one 'hiding in the walk-in fridge'. These words all work together to suggest a sharp contrast between organised, brave, successful US troops and a weak, ineffectual purposeless opposition.

4 Choose three of the highlighted words or phrases in the article and explain the meaning and effect of each one.

**Phalanx** means an organised troop of soldiers in a battle formation. The effect is to add to the image of the US soldiers as competent and orderly. **hectares** of marble flooring means huge areas covered in marble stone. This is hyperbole, suggesting that Saddam Hussein has decorated his palaces opulently, using marble, a very expensive material. The effect is that it makes the reader begin to comprehend the extravagant size and grandeur of the palaces. **faux antique** means a pretend antique, something built recently to look as if it is from a particular period in the past. By describing the chair like this the journalist implies that Hussein's world is one of imitations and it links to the 'imitation French baroque' furniture mentioned further on in the article – the furniture is not even Iraqi. **freakin'** is a slang word to replace a common expletive and means 'absolutely' in this phrase – 'the city is absolutely ours now'. It is used in a quotation from one of the US soldiers and makes him seem calm and casual and feeling in charge. It also gives a personal touch by using an adjective used in common speech. **"triumph"** The word means victory but it is used ironically to mock Saddam Hussein. He did not really win the Gulf War. He may have thought it a victory because he became the dictator in Iraq but it was not a real victory. The use of inverted commas around the word shows the reader it is used ironically. **confection** means something like confectionery, a sweet cake or sweets. It is used to suggest that the New Presidential Palace is over the top, that it looks like a wedding cake or something you would see in a fancy cake shop. It adds to the article's presentation of Hussein's taste as extreme, a bit foolish or in bad taste. **hooked on glitz** is a colloquial phrase, which means addicted to shiny showy things. It is linked to the list of Saddam Hussein's interior furnishings like fake antique furniture and gold taps. It is designed to suggest he did not have good taste and wasted lots of money.

ISBN 9780170233293

**autocrat** means a ruler who rules alone and for his own ends. The noun is used to emphasise the way Saddam Hussein allowed no-one to soften his personal search for wealth and pleasure while the people he ruled starved.

All of these answers are fine. They explain the meaning of and address the effect of the phrase in terms of the whole article.

5 In the poem, Shelley quotes the words written at the base of the statue and the journalist uses these words, too. Explain in your own words the irony in the meaning of these words and their link with the newspaper piece's theme.

"My name is Ozymandias, king of kings: Look on my works ye mighty and despair!"

When the statue was built, Ozymandias was ruler of a great empire and is telling his foes how strong and powerful he is. The words are now ironic because that empire lies in ruins, destroyed and the imperative now directs us to see how he is not strong and powerful any longer.

This links with the article because Saddam Hussein believed he was all-powerful but has been removed from power and is described as 'Iraq's own crumbling pharaoh'. The adjective 'crumbling' is particularly good as it relates both to modern Iraq and the statue's decaying stone shape.

In Ozymandias's case it is time that has destroyed his kingdom; for Hussein it is the US troops but both pieces deal with the idea that a tyrant will eventually be deposed.

This answer is a strong one. It deals with both parts of the question and supports the points the student makes with quotation and reference to the text, as well as using technical terms correctly.

6 This article might be said to be biased or written from a particular standpoint. Why might this be? How can you tell?

This could be biased because of a number of different reasons. It is possible that perhaps the writer was a victim of some of the crimes that Saddam committed, or that the writer has an intense dislike of Saddam Hussein and Iraq. It is also possible that the writer is only allowed to write certain things, and this is the


ISBN 9780170233293

information that they have been given. Bias is seen throughout the article as Milmo does not mention anything positive about Saddam in the article yet nothing negative is said about the American soldiers, even when they stole Saddam Hussein's personal items.

The first two sentences here do not answer the question at all. The student probably knows this as they use 'could', 'possible' and 'perhaps' and seem to be thinking things out in writing. In the final two sentences the student begins to respond.

The answer must relate to the article and must address both parts.

**Consider:**

The writer has been present and must have permission to be there so perhaps he is an 'embedded' reporter. He knows the names of some US soldiers and has talked with them. It uses positive language ('comrades' etc) to describe them and, as the student says, does not criticise them at all. It seems to be written therefore from a Western (even US) point of view.

The article stresses the inadequacy of the opposition, the extravagance and wastefulness of the Hussein regime and its lack of care for ordinary Iraqi citizens.

It uses many terms to ridicule Hussein himself – 'latter day Saladin' and 'vanquisher of the crusade armies' etc.

The article does not mention any Iraqi opinion, and does not say how the US soldiers met the minimal resistance.

This final response needs to offer some idea of the overall tone of the piece and the writer's attitude to the subject.

We hope that this look at a student response to a close reading piece has shown you how important it is that you read and understand the whole work before you begin to look at it in more detail.

- You see what it is about.
- You respond to its tone and message.
- You look more closely at its construction.

Then your responses to the particular questions will help you to interpret, evaluate and discuss the author's methods of conveying meaning to you as you arrive at a greater understanding of the work.

# 8 Connections Across Texts

Achievement Standard 3.7 *Respond critically to significant connections across texts, supported by evidence* is the culmination of all the study in English you have been doing for the past few years. Your English teachers have been helping you to understand fully what you read and to appreciate the skills of good writers. In this Standard you will be expected to use your skills of analysis to link texts.

This Standard also gives you the wonderful opportunity to

choose for yourself

the texts to be connected, provided of course that they are at the right level.

AND it involves everything you have learnt to do in English in the last five years at high school. Close reading, understanding poetry, analysing films, following novelists' themes and motifs, observing short story structures, making presentations, studying media items, using the Internet well, writing literary essays ...

**An aside on ... thinking for yourself**

AS 3.7 requires critical and original thinking. Here are two Year 13 students talking about Year 13 English ... who is likely to write the better essay?

'Hamlet's a mess. It's full of inconsistencies. For a start, Hamlet should be king himself, once his father's dead. He's old enough, surely? Or do you reckon that Shakespeare meant him to be a teenager? That would explain nearly everything, if he was a young teenager – younger than us. Those young kids are mad – like Finnegan in the lower fifth. I mean, Finnigan's capable of anything. So why do they use people like Olivier to play Hamlet? Should be somebody like Mick Jagger, only younger. Then it would all make sense.'

But you can't put that in an essay!'

'Don't see why not. It's the truth.'

'The examiners would crucify you.'

'You believe in the safe answer, then? Giving the examiners what they expect? The examiners tell the accepted truth to the teachers, and the teachers tell us, and then we tell the examiners. What a bloody waste of time.'



ISBN 9780170233293

By now you know how to be a good judge: how to be critical, perceptive, insightful. You know what sort of information you need to draw from a text of any kind to be able to answer questions about it to reveal your understanding.

The best responses to this Standard will be the ones you have thought of yourself, not the repeat of ones other people have told you. It's time to participate in your own education. As we said, this is where you get to choose!

Yes, you need to select text of the appropriate level. It's not a time for Hairy Maclary (unless you are studying the linguistics of children's literature), but in general you get to choose!

During Year 13 you have spent a considerable amount of time looking at shorter texts. You have read, analysed, answered questions on text in isolation. You have compared texts, looked for similarities and differences; you have made connections between shorter texts in this book and probably in your classroom too. NCEA Level 3 expects you to be able to look at each text and what connects them with a critical eye. This does not mean to criticise negatively but to examine what the writer is saying, how they are saying it and whether they are saying it well.

The best responses are those where the student has really thought about the texts: carefully considered the connections, which might be ideas and/or structures and/or techniques used, and offered a judgement based on those thoughts.

If you look at the assessment criteria you will see words like:

| | |
|---|---|
| **Convincingly** | which means **persuasively, believably, realistically** |
| **Perceptive** | which means **understanding, observant, discerning, aware** |
| **Discerning** | which means **discriminating, sharp, astute** |
| **Informed** | which means **knowledgeable, conversant, learned** |
| **Sophisticated** | which means **complex, mature, highly developed, grown-up** |
| **Insightful** | which means **understanding, perceptive, aware** |

and the most challenging of all ...

| | |
|---|---|
| **Original** | which means **new, unique, creative, inventive, imaginative, special** |

These tell you what the marker is looking for.

In other words, your writing should convince the marker that you understand completely what you have read, that you have made reasoned and reasonable connections between the texts and that you have rational opinions about these connections.

This could be FUN!

ISBN 9780170233293

## Choosing your texts

Your teacher will most likely give you some guidance on this. In fact it is likely that you will be able to use some of the texts you have studied in class.

At this stage don't limit yourself to only three or four texts. This is the 'brainstorm' stage. Have as many as you can so that you can play with the connections between them.

1. Start with at least one text that you have studied in class. Why? Because you know it well, you have already formed opinions, have notes, developed essays etc.
2. Look at all the other texts you have studied in class and see if you can pull something else from your year's work. It could be a film, a poem or an extract from a close reading.
3. Look at other books or poems these authors have written.
4. Look at the books you have read personally. Do any of these fit with those texts you have already chosen?
5. Think of films that you have both studied and seen outside of school.
6. Think of texts you have studied in previous years. Would any of these fit?
7. Think of texts you have heard your peers have studied. Would any of these fit?
8. Talk to your teacher.
9. Talk to your librarian (both school and local public library).
10. Talk to your parents.
11. Talk to your friends.


ISBN 9780170233293

## What might create a connection?

Think about the usual things you study: subject, character, setting, theme. There will be lots of other possibilities and ways to make connections across different texts. You might choose to look at:

**SUBJECT**

- aeroplanes
- computers
- dance
- exploration
- fashion
- fishing
- horses
- motorbikes
- mountaineering
- music
- parents
- politics
- rugby
- school
- soccer
- social networking
- surfing
- theatre

**CHARACTER**

- a life story, or a particular time in a person's life like school days or holiday time
- a teenage girl as the central character, or an elderly male, or a young child, or a young man
  - a daughter
  - a grandfather
  - a mother

**NARRATIVE STYLE**

- first person narrator
- third person eye-of-god (author tells what every character thinks and feels as well as does and says)
- third person from just one character's perspective

**THEME**

- ambition
- conflict
- courage
- family
- fear
- friendship
- greed
- growing up
- hope
- love
- loyalty
- prejudice

**GENRE**

- adventure
- chic-lit
- gothic
- historical fiction
- horror
- romance
- science fiction
- survival stories
- thriller

**SETTING**

**TIME**

- a historical period:
  - colonial New Zealand
  - Tudor England
  - ancient Rome
- the future
- wartime
- during or just after a disaster

**PLACE**

- a specific location:
  - Christchurch
  - London
  - Wellington
  - Australia
  - South Africa
- or a general location:
  - in the bush
  - mountains
  - the beach
  - a city
  - the country
  - small town life
  - a new place

**SOCIAL BACKGROUND**

- poverty
- wealth
- class differences (upstairs/downstairs)
- male/female
- racial grouping
  - African American
  - Māori
  - Pacific Island
  - indigenous peoples
  - Scottish migrants
  - displaced people

ISBN 9780170233293

# Connecting texts

We have looked at comparing two texts. Now we take three texts and ask you to examine each one, then look for connections between them.

## Text 1

This passage is an extract from *Pride and Prejudice* by Jane Austen. Read the passage several times. As you do so, highlight:

- Effective adjectives or adverbs or verbs
- Figurative language
- Repetition
- Significant syntax.

### Chapter One

It is a truth universally acknowledged, that a single man in possession of a good fortune, must be in want of a wife.

However little known the feelings or views of such a man may be on his first entering a neighbourhood, this truth is so well fixed in the minds of the surrounding families that he is considered as the rightful property of some one or other of their daughters.

"My dear Mr. Bennet," said his lady to him one day, "have you heard that Netherfield Park is let at last?"

Mr. Bennet replied that he had not.

"But it is," returned she; "for Mrs. Long has just been here, and she told me all about it."

Mr. Bennet made no answer.

"Do not you want to know who has taken it?" cried his wife impatiently.

"*You* want to tell me, and I have no objection to hearing it."

This was invitation enough.

"Why, my dear, you must know, Mrs. Long says that Netherfield is taken by a young man of large fortune from the north of England; that he came down on Monday in a chaise and four to see the place, and was so much delighted with it, that he agreed with Mr. Morris immediately; that he is to take possession before Michaelmas, and some of his servants are to be in the house by the end of next week."

"What is his name?"

"Bingley."

"Is he married or single?"

"Oh! single, my dear, to be sure! A single man of large fortune; four or five thousand a year. What a fine thing for our girls!"

"How so? how can it affect them?"

"My dear Mr. Bennet," replied his wife, "how can you be so tiresome! You must know that I am thinking of his marrying one of them."

"Is that his design in settling here?"

"Design! nonsense, how can you talk so! But it is very likely that he *may* fall in love with one of them, and therefore you must visit him as soon as he comes."

"I see no occasion for that. You and the girls may go, or you may send them by themselves, which perhaps will be still better, for as you are as handsome as any of them, Mr. Bingley might like you the best of the party."



ISBN 9780170233293

"My dear, you flatter me. I certainly *have* had my share of beauty, but I do not pretend to be any thing extraordinary now. When a woman has five grown-up daughters she ought to give over thinking of her own beauty."

"In such cases a woman has not often much beauty to think of."

"But, my dear, you must indeed go and see Mr. Bingley when he comes into the neighbourhood."

"It is more than I engage for, I assure you."

"But consider your daughters. Only think what an establishment it would be for one of them. Sir William and Lady Lucas are determined to go, merely on that account, for in general, you know, they visit no new-comers. Indeed you must go, for it will be impossible for us to visit him if you do not."

"You are over-scrupulous surely. I dare say Mr. Bingley will be very glad to see you; and I will send a few lines by you to assure him of my hearty consent to his marrying whichever he chuses of the girls: though I must throw in a good word for my little Lizzy."

"I desire you will do no such thing. Lizzy is not a bit better than the others; and I am sure she is not half so handsome as Jane, nor half so good-humoured as Lydia. But you are always giving *her* the preference."

"They have none of them much to recommend them," replied he; "they are all silly and ignorant, like other girls; but Lizzy has something more of quickness than her sisters."

"Mr. Bennet, how can you abuse your own children in such a way! You take delight in vexing me. You have no compassion on my poor nerves."

"You mistake me, my dear. I have a high respect for your nerves. They are my old friends. I have heard you mention them with consideration these twenty years at least."

"Ah! you do not know what I suffer."

"But I hope you will get over it, and live to see many young men of four thousand a year come into the neighbourhood."

"It will be no use to us if twenty such should come, since you will not visit them."

"Depend upon it, my dear, that when there are twenty, I will visit them all."

Mr. Bennet was so odd a mixture of quick parts, sarcastic humour, reserve, and caprice, that the experience of three-and-twenty years had been insufficient to make his wife understand his character. *Her* mind was less difficult to develop. She was a woman of mean understanding, little information, and uncertain temper. When she was discontented she fancied herself nervous. The business of her life was to get her daughters married; its solace was visiting and news.

**Answer the following questions in as much detail as possible. Use quotations and references to the text to support your ideas.**

1 What do you NOT know about Mr and Mrs Bennet? Why are these details not provided?

ISBN 9780170233293

2 What DO you know about Mr and Mrs Bennet? Use the author's final paragraph to help you sort out your answer.

3 The first chapter mentions several other people. Who? What do we learn about them? Who is likely to be important?

4 The opening paragraph is clearly ironic – young wealthy men do not need wives. The paragraph tells us several things about the story that will follow. What are they?


ISBN 9780170233293

## Text 2

This passage is an extract from *A Farewell to Arms* by Earnest Hemingway. The novel is set in Italy, during World War One. Read the passage several times. As you do so, highlight:

- Effective adjectives or adverbs or verbs
- Figurative language
- Repetition
- Significant syntax.

### Chapter One

In the late summer of that year we lived in a village that looked across the river and the plain to the mountains. In the bed of the river there were pebbles and boulders, dry and white in the sun, and the water was clear and swiftly moving and blue in the channels. Troops went by the house and down the road and the dust they raised powdered the leaves of the trees. The trunks of the trees too were dusty and the leaves fell early that year and we saw the troops marching along the road and the dust rising and leaves, stirred by the breeze, falling and the soldiers marching and afterwards the road bare and white except for the leaves.

The plain was rich with crops; there were many orchards of fruit trees and beyond the plain the mountains were brown and bare. There was fighting in the mountains and at night we could see the flashes from the artillery. In the dark it was like summer lightning, but the nights were cool and there was not the feeling of storm coming.

Sometimes in the dark we heard the troops marching under the window and guns going past pulled by motor-tractors. Here was much traffic at night and many mules on the roads with boxes of ammunition on each side of their pack-saddles and grey motor-trucks that carried men, and other trucks with loads covered with canvas that moved slower in the traffic. There were big guns too that passed in the day drawn by tractors, the long barrels of guns covered with green branches and green leafy branches and vines laid over the tractors. To the north we could look across a valley and see a forest of chestnut trees and behind it another mountain on this side of the river. There was fighting for that mountain too, but it was not successful, and in the fall when the rains came the leaves all fell from the chestnut trees and the branches were bare and the trunks black with rain. The vineyards were thin and bare-branched too and all the country wet and brown and dead with the autumn. There were mists over the river and clouds on the mountain and the trucks splashed mud on the roads and the troops were muddy and wet in their capes; their rifles were wet and under their capes the two leather cartridge-boxes on the front of the belts, grey leather boxes heavy with the packs of clips of thin, long 6.5 mm. cartridges, bulged forward under the capes so that the men, passing on the road, marched as though they were six months gone with child. There were small grey motor-cars that passed going very fast; usually there was an officer on the seat with the driver and more officers in the back seat. They splashed more mud than the camions* even and if one of the officers in the back was very small and sitting between two generals, he himself so small that you could not see his face but only the top of his cap and his narrow back, and if the car went especially fast it was probably the King. He lived in Udine and came out in this way nearly every day to see how things were going, and things went very badly.

At the start of the winter came the permanent rain and with the rain came the cholera. But it was checked and in the end only seven thousand died of it in the army.

ISBN 9780170233293

**Answer the following question in as much detail as possible. Use quotations and references to the text to support your ideas.**

1 Choose two of the techniques you have highlighted examples of and explain why the writer has used them.

Technique 1: ______

______

______

Technique 2: ______

______

______

**Now that you have considered the author's choice of vocabulary and style, answer the following questions in as much detail as possible.**

2 Briefly, what do you know about the narrator?

______

______

______

______

______

3 What does the narrator notice about the natural world he is living in?

______

______

______

______

______

4 What is the narrator's attitude to the war?

______

______

______

______



ISBN 9780170233293

5 Why, do you think, has the writer chosen to open this novel with these words?

## Text 3

This passage is an extract from *Great Expectations* by Charles Dickens. This novel was first published in serial form in a newspaper. You could compare this with the first episode of a TV drama. Read the passage several times. As you do so, highlight:

- Effective adjectives or adverbs or verbs
- Figurative language
- Repetition
- Significant syntax.

### Chapter One

MY FATHER'S FAMILY name being Pirrip, and my Christian name Philip, my infant tongue could make of both names nothing longer or more explicit than Pip. So, I called myself Pip, and came to be called Pip.

I give Pirrip as my father's family name, on the authority of his tombstone and my sister—Mrs. Joe Gargery, who married the blacksmith. As I never saw my father or my mother, and never saw any likeness of either of them (for their days were long before the days of photographs), my first fancies regarding what they were like, were unreasonably derived from their tombstones. The shape of the letters on my father's gave me an odd idea that he was a square, stout, dark man, with curly black hair. From the character and turn of the inscription, "Also Georgiana Wife of the Above," I drew a childish conclusion that my mother was freckled and sickly. To five little stone lozenges, each about a foot and a half long, which were arranged in a neat row beside their grave, and were sacred to the memory of five little brothers of mine—who gave up trying to get a living exceedingly early in that universal struggle—I am indebted for a belief I religiously entertained that they had all been born on their backs with their hands in their trousers-pockets, and had never taken them out in this state of existence.

ISBN 9780170233293

Ours was the marsh country, down by the river, within, as the river wound, twenty miles of the sea. My first most vivid and broad impression of the identity of things, seems to me to have been gained on a memorable raw afternoon towards evening. At such a time I found out for certain, that this bleak place overgrown with nettles was the churchyard; and that Philip Pirrip, late of this parish, and also Georgiana wife of the above, were dead and buried; and that Alexander, Bartholomew, Abraham, Tobias, and Roger, infant children of the aforesaid, were also dead and buried; and that the dark flat wilderness beyond the churchyard, intersected with dykes and mounds and gates, with scattered cattle feeding on it, was the marshes; and that the low leaden line beyond was the river; and that the distant savage lair from which the wind was rushing, was the sea; and that the small bundle of shivers growing afraid of it all and beginning to cry, was Pip.

"Hold your noise!" cried a terrible voice, as a man started up from among the graves at the side of the church porch. "Keep still, you little devil, or I'll cut your throat!"

A fearful man, all in coarse grey, with a great iron on his leg. A man with no hat, and with broken shoes, and with an old rag tied round his head. A man who had been soaked in water, and smothered in mud, and lamed by stones, and cut by flints, and stung by nettles, and torn by briars; who limped, and shivered, and glared and growled; and whose teeth chattered in his head as he seized me by the chin.

"O! Don't cut my throat, sir," I pleaded in terror. "Pray don't do it, sir."

The rest of this chapter is available in the book itself or on the Internet. We suggest you read it all.

**Answer the following question in as much detail as possible. Use quotations and references to the text to support your ideas.**

1 How does the author capture the reader's interest in this opening chapter?

You might mention use of dialogue, introduction of character/s, description of setting, use of an incident, creation of mood, use of humour.



ISBN 9780170233293

## Making connections

Now, think about all three texts. Using what you have observed of the writers' techniques, and thinking about where each of these passages comes within each novel, draw some conclusions about the way these writers have chosen to absorb their reader, to keep their reader from closing this book (or e-reader) and continuing to read. Note any similarities and differences between them in terms of the techniques they use.

ISBN 9780170233293

# Other things that might help

## The Internet ...

Searching the web for links in literature can work really well. We tried it with dystopian literature and here is part of what we got ...

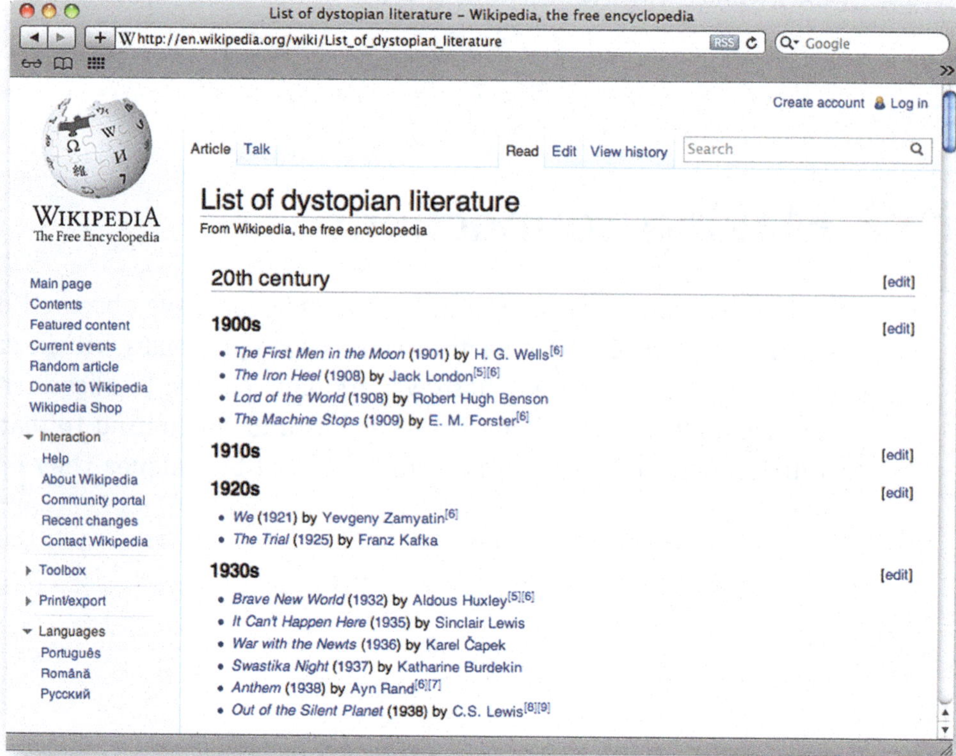
List of dystopian literature – Wikipedia, the free encyclopedia

http://en.wikipedia.org/wiki/List_of_dystopian_literature

Create account Log in

Article Talk Read Edit View history Search

WIKIPEDIA
The Free Encyclopedia

Main page
Contents
Featured content
Current events
Random article
Donate to Wikipedia
Wikipedia Shop
Interaction
Help
About Wikipedia
Community portal
Recent changes
Contact Wikipedia
Toolbox
Print/export
Languages
Português
Română
Русский

**List of dystopian literature**

From Wikipedia, the free encyclopedia

**20th century** [edit]

**1900s** [edit]

- *The First Men in the Moon* (1901) by H. G. Wells[6]
- *The Iron Heel* (1908) by Jack London[5][6]
- *Lord of the World* (1908) by Robert Hugh Benson
- *The Machine Stops* (1909) by E. M. Forster[6]

**1910s** [edit]

**1920s** [edit]

- *We* (1921) by Yevgeny Zamyatin[6]
- *The Trial* (1925) by Franz Kafka

**1930s** [edit]

- *Brave New World* (1932) by Aldous Huxley[5][6]
- *It Can't Happen Here* (1935) by Sinclair Lewis
- *War with the Newts* (1936) by Karel Čapek
- *Swastika Night* (1937) by Katharine Burdekin
- *Anthem* (1938) by Ayn Rand[6][7]
- *Out of the Silent Planet* (1938) by C.S. Lewis[8][9]

## A book ...

People like to write lists ... some have written lists of books that are worth reading. Recently in New Zealand, Jim Flynn, a professor at the University of Otago, wrote *The Torchlight List*. Here is part of a review ...

> Professor Jim Flynn is one of the smartest and most interesting people I have met.
>
> He blames modern day teenage culture for creating a vocabulary gap and a love-of-reading deficit. His solution is to read extensively, with curiosity and for fun.
>
> 'I want them to be able to understand the world, rather than just be swept along by the river of time with no real comprehension of what is happening to them.'
>
> The book is well subtitled. It is indeed a type of round-the-world trip traversing the histories and cultures of America, Latin America, Britain and its colonies, the European power houses, Africa and Asia. Each chapter gives a little background information while using a summary of the best books and authors to continue the story. It makes frank suggestions of what Flynn believes to be the very best reading, both fact and fiction on each region as well as suggestions for reading on the human condition.
>
> From F Scott Fitzgerald on American mortality to Robert Fisk on the West's intervention in the Middle East, Japanese pop culture's Haruki Murakami to our own Janet Frame – listed here are 200 books to be discovered and enjoyed.

The choice is yours ...
go on have some fun! WE DARE YOU!



ISBN 9780170233293

# Writing a Good Essay

At NCEA Level 3 you may be required to complete several extended written responses to a variety of text as part of your external assessments. Depending on your school's syllabus these texts may be written, visual or oral.

**Written text**

- novel
- non-fiction
- Non-shakespearean drama script
- Shakespearean drama script
- short story
- poetry
- song lyric
- print media
- digital
- online
- or a combination of the above (intertextual studies).

**Visual or oral text**

- film
- television programme
- drama production
- radio programme
- oral performance
- multi-media
- graphic novel
- digital
- online
- or a combination of the above (intertextual studies).

**You will be expected to ...**

- have read/viewed/listened and studied the work/s in class
- structure a critical response
- offer supporting evidence by using specific and relevant details from your text
- produce a personally thoughtful response to the text/s.

**You will be asked to compose your critical response in a particular format:**

Write an essay with:

- an introduction
- a range of points logically linked to each other and to your introduction
- a reasoned conclusion that draws from the points you make in the body of your essay
- accurate use and control of writing conventions.

ISBN 9780170233293

### Questions are likely to relate to:

- purpose and audience
- ideas (e.g. character, theme, setting)
- language features (e.g. figurative language, syntax, style, symbolism, diction, vocabulary, sound devices)
- structures (e.g. narrative sequence, beginnings and endings).

#### An aside on ... critical response

The examiner's instruction at this level requires you to provide a 'critical response'. Sometimes students think that this means that they are being asked to criticise (ie find fault with) a text or texts. However, in this sense of textual criticism, you are being asked to show that you understand the text you have studied by delivering an analysis and perhaps a judgement on the work of an author by offering explanations of the writer's way of creating his or her ideas and your opinion of his/her success. You have been doing similar things for several years now in your English classes; at Year 13 you will study more sophisticated text and be expected to write at greater length, with more sophistication in your own use of language and depth of understanding and appreciation.

#### An aside on ... you have the skills

You have studied short texts in class as preparation for your close reading of unfamiliar written text assessments. This has taught you to look closely at how a passage has been created for meaning and effect. You have looked for such things as vocabulary choice, tone, interesting syntax, figures of speech etc and you will find all of these same techniques being used by writers when you read a longer text like a novel ... especially the second time you read the text.

The long answer on an unfamiliar text is in essence no different from the essay answer on a longer text you have studied in class for six weeks.

Annotation of a longer text helps, too. If you own the book, or if you are able to photocopy significant pages, then annotate on the book itself as you read, in the same way as you have done for shorter text passages.

## Writing an essay

Writing a formal essay for English uses the same skills that writing an essay for any other subject does. You will:

- find the information that you need
- evaluate it and decide what you will use
- construct a clear and logical argument based on the topic.

So you are showing the skills of **research, thinking** and **communicating** when you present an essay for assessment.


ISBN 9780170233293

### What makes a good essay?

A good essay will:

- show evidence of research – beyond what was offered in class, perhaps
- show that the writer (you!) has an opinion or ideas about the topic
- show a clear and logical structure
- show use of example and evidence in support of the ideas and opinions expressed
- show the writer's ability to use writing conventions accurately.

### Why do I have to keep writing essays?

If you want to play rugby well, or netball, or golf, or chess or PlayStation what do you do? You prepare, you train, you practise. It's the same for writing (and thinking, and speaking, and well ... everything really). If you want to get better at doing something you need to work at it.

Practice makes perfect. It's an old saying and still a true one.

# The practicalities: preparation, writing and presentation

## 1 Preparation

It is expected that you have **thought about the topic yourself** and that you will express your own ideas, supported by evidence from the text. You do not have to agree with your teacher, but your ideas must be supported by the text! Think about what might contradict you. Obviously you need to know the text well, a single read through is often insufficient. If you are serious about doing well you need to read/view any long text at least twice and a short one several times.

**Read the question carefully.**

- Identify the instruction words: eg, *comment, explain, describe, compare, contrast*, etc.
- Identify the content words: eg, *film, poet, Shakespeare, novel, conflict.*
- Identify any limiting words: eg, *New Zealand literature, 20th century, two.*
- Questions often have two parts to them and both must be addressed in the essay.
- Be clear on the meaning of the question before you begin. Sometimes it can be useful to express the topic in your own words to ensure that you understand it before you begin to write.
- Classroom notes should help you and you may find works of criticism that help, too. Your teacher may have given you a reading list. Take notes from your reading as you go. You will probably have to include a bibliography (see page 120) for class essays.
- If you use the exact words written by someone else about your text, you must acknowledge this by placing them in inverted commas and identifying where the reference comes from. If you just copy from a source such as a book or the Internet, this is plagiarism.

ISBN 9780170233293

- Plan the essay:
  - list all the main points you wish to make
  - arrange them in a logical order
  - link your ideas
  - make sure you have evidence from the text (references and quotations) to support your ideas.

**Time management is crucial**

- You need to allocate enough time to do the additional reading that might be needed, the thinking, the planning, the drafting, the good copy for handing in.
- In other words, beginning on Sunday night before a Monday morning deadline is not a great idea.

## Are you a procrastinator?

If you don't know what this word means, look it up. There are dictionaries online, in the library, in your English classroom, on your parents' bookshelf, in your bedroom. Use one: often!

**Here are some tactics to help you:**

| Plan and prioritise: |
|---|
| Tackle the most important tasks first, eg, do the reading, make notes, plan the essay, write the first draft, proof, write the final draft. |
| Begin well before the deadline. |
| Write an easy part first. |
| Make a list of ideas, do a mind map, a brainstorm. |
| Tell someone who cares and ask for their supportive interest. |
| Bribe yourself eg, half an hour of TV for two pages of words. |
| Write a minimum number of words every time you begin: at least 100. |
| Ask your teacher to look at your plan or draft. Accept constructive criticism. |
| Work when you are at your best. 5 am? 8 pm? Few people work really well late at night! |
| Have a recognised work-station; a desk is ideal, but your corner of the dining table works, too. |

| Useful techniques include: |
|---|
| Recording relevant quotations on cards, in colours, with page number or line for easy location or use Post-it notes on the actual text. |
| Making notes on sections of the essay on different pieces of paper. |
| Highlighting relevant points from class notes. |
| Making pencil notes in the text (if it is allowed). |
| Taking note of a critic's ideas. Be sure to acknowledge any such source though, to avoid plagiarism. |
| Use language that you understand and do not be tempted into 'padding' to achieve greater length. A straightforward, economical expression of your ideas is what you are aiming for. |
| Write a minimum number of words every time you begin: at least 100. |
| Ask your teacher to look at your plan or draft. Accept constructive criticism. |


ISBN 9780170233293

## 2 Writing

Begin your essay with an introductory paragraph that outlines *briefly* the steps of your argument and your own approach to the topic.

Develop your ideas in paragraph format, dealing with each new idea in a new paragraph. Your final paragraph should be a conclusion, a summary of the ideas already presented.

As you write your first draft you will discover what you know, and what you need to know. Read your own work critically. Ask yourself:

- Can I see my key sentences in my paragraphs?
- Have I used examples to support an idea?
- Have I used quotations to support my ideas?
- Have I incorporated explanations and evaluations of my ideas?
- Have I been persuasive?

## 3 Presentation

**Type or write** on one side of A4 paper. Leave a 5 cm margin on one side for comments. Writing longhand rather than typing the essay can be useful as the examination will be handwritten and it's easy to get out of practice, both in writing for a long time and in judging the length of an essay. However, a marker must be able to read what you write. Legibility of handwriting is important.

**Proofread carefully.**

- Check **spelling** – especially of names of authors, titles and characters. Nothing makes you seem more careless than being unable to spell a writer's name!
- Check **paragraphing** – they should be used to group your ideas. (Some students seem to think it necessary to separate their writing into evenly sized sections!)
- Check **punctuation** – at this level you should be able to use correctly the apostrophe, colon, semi-colon, parentheses (brackets). If you are unsure, consult a good dictionary or grammar text.
- Check **tense** – be sure that you are consistent.
- Check the **logical order** of your ideas.
- Underline **titles** of text, place all **quotations** in inverted commas. Use a forward slash to show quoting over a line of poetry. When quoting full lines of poetry, centre justify the quotation.
- Do not use **slang** or colloquial expressions. Avoid **abbreviations.**

**Editing**

One really useful thing to do is have someone read your work before you hand it in. They can often find errors in accuracy or gaps in content that the writer has missed. We tend to read what we *think* we've written.

ISBN 9780170233293

## An aside on ... references and bibliographies

When you quote from a text the simplest thing to do is to put brackets after the quotation with the author's name, year of publication, page number, e.g. (Thomas and White 2003: 22-23), and then add the name of the text in your bibliography like this:

1 Name of author/s followed by a full stop.
2 Date of publication of the book in brackets.
3 The title of the book underlined (titles in print are in italics). Use quotation marks for a short story or an article or poem – things that would not be published on their own.
4 City of publication followed by a colon.
5 Name of publisher.

**Example: handwritten**

J. Thomas and D. White. (2003) Achievement English at Year 12 Auckland: New House Publishers

**Example: in print**

J. Thomas and D. White. (2003) *Achievement English at Year 12 Auckland:* New House Publishers

# 4 Post-essay (to rewrite or not to rewrite?)

### Feedback

Teacher feedback is immensely valuable. The work that you do in preparation for your final assessment writing is important and your teacher will help you to improve your writing throughout the year. The essay that you write at the end of the year will be better than the one you write at the beginning because your teacher will guide you. Do as good a job as possible with each essay you write in order to have comments that will help improve your writing as much as possible before your final assessment.

### Peer support

Reading essays by other students can assist you to improve your own writing as you observe different ways of approaching a topic. This goes for bad ones as well as good ones. You will not copy another person's work – this is plagiarism – but any writer will tell you that the way to improve your own writing is to read the writing of others.

Remember, these essays are representing your finest attempt at expressing your own ideas in your own words.


ISBN 9780170233293

# What next?

You've read the novel.

You've talked about it in class.

You've thought about its characters, events, ideas, themes, structure.

You've got a topic.

**Now what?**

One thing students can sometimes struggle with is deciding what to write and although it is difficult to help in a book like this because all students will be using different texts and all students will write differently, we can give you some guidelines about how to decide what you want in your personal response to the text(s) you have studied in class.

What separates a Level 3 essay from the ones you have written in previous years is that you are expected to explore, in greater detail and depth, more sophisticated ideas..

Let's take a step back and look at a simple example from an earlier level of study. A student answered a question on *Romeo and Juliet*:

**QUESTION:**

*Who is responsible for the deaths of the star-crossed lovers?*

ISBN 9780170233293

| | Explanations | Examples |
|---|---|---|
| **Superficial answer**<br>A basic answer which most likely uses simplistic idea/s and supporting material. | The parents (Lord/Lady Capulet, Lord/Lady Montague) … because it was they who continued, or at least allowed the continuation of, the feud.<br>**Note:**<br>In particular Capulet as he was the one who forced Juliet into marriage (to Paris) which made her take such drastic measures. | Fighting in the streets and both men wanting to join in.<br>Having a party where the other was not welcome.<br>"have you delivered our decree?" 3.5<br>"Hang thee, young baggage, disobedient wretch … get thee to church or never after look me in the face." 3.5 |
| **More detailed answer**<br>An answer which clearly covers the question on more than a general level. The student will have understood that there is more than a single response and will use several supporting references. | As above and …<br>The parents …<br>detachment from children. They are unaware what is going on in their children's lives.<br>Romeo & Juliet …<br>personal responsibility for their rash behaviour.<br>Friar Laurence/Nurse …<br>was their guidance/advice sensible? … was it responsible to help cover up the young lovers actions to the extent they did? | At the beginning Montague does not understand his son's behaviour. Capulet does not listen to Juliet's view of marriage to Paris.<br>They did not think of the consequences of their actions, nor the speed of their actions etc. Had an idealistic outcome.<br>Both helped to deceive parents … the Nurse in particular. The Friar dabbling in herbal medicines and using them for the purpose of deception etc. |
| **In-depth answer**<br>This student will have taken the question a step further. They will admit there are other factors involved. | As above and …<br>Fate/Chance …<br>played a significant part in the action. It was merely a series of misadventures.<br>Social Responsibility/Context …<br>Romeo and Juliet live in a world where a feud such as this allowed to continue. | Letter being waylaid, Juliet awakening only moments too late etc.<br>"Star crossed lovers" Prologue<br>"Set my sail" "in the stars." 1.4<br>Servants and employees are willing to carry on the feud. i.e. "biting their thumb" in the first scene. |


ISBN 9780170233293

You will be asked a more sophisticated question about your text at this level, but if you follow a similar process for your text you will be able to see how your answer can be developed at a more advanced level.

Use the following template to help you plan an essay for a text you are studying in class.

| | |
|---|---|
| Title of text: | |
| Author of text: | |
| Type of text: | |
| Question: | |

Use this space to help you with your planning.

ISBN 9780170233293

| | Explanations | Examples |
|---|---|---|
| **Superficial answer**<br>A basic answer which most likely uses simplistic idea/s and supporting material. | | |
| **More detailed answer**<br>An answer which clearly covers the question on more than a general level. The student will have understood that there is more than a single response and will use several supporting references. | | |
| **In-depth answer**<br>This student will have taken the question a step further. They will admit there are other factors involved. | | |



ISBN 9780170233293

## An aside on ... using quotations effectively

By this stage of your career as a writer of essays you should be confident in your use of quotations. You should be able to use them to illustrate the points you are making, to support your ideas, rather than just repeating yourself.

Part of the sophistication and depth required at this level is being able to incorporate your quotations into your essay. Here are a few guidelines to help you:

- Put inverted commas at the beginning and the end of the quotation. These show exactly which words are not yours.
- Keep quotations short. If they are short you will be more likely to remember them to use in assessments/exams.
- Be accurate. Use and learn the words exactly as they are used. If you cannot remember them, then paraphrase.
- Quotations should not repeat basic facts already given. Compare these two uses of the same quotation:

  a In Catcher in the Rye by JD Salinger, the narrator, Holden Caulfield, tells us that he is not going to tell us his life story. 'I'm not going to tell you my whole goddam autobiography or anything.'

  b In Catcher in the Rye by JD Salinger, the narrator, Holden Caulfield, insists: 'I'm not going to tell you my whole goddam autobiography or anything.'

- Try to embed the quotation into the sentence to embellish the point you are making – this is a more sophisticated technique.

  Holden tells us on the first page that his story will reveal a part of his life that has been disturbing: 'this madman stuff that happened to me last Christmas.'

- Quotations can support your ideas.

  Holden is a teenager; his use of slang 'kind of crap' and exaggeration when referring to his parents 'My parents would have about two haemorrhages apiece ...' reveals his likely age and defensive attitude.

- Quoting from poetry – and this includes much of Shakespeare – requires you to follow certain conventions. Centre the quotation if it is of more than two lines of verse.

  After the fight at the beginning of Romeo and Juliet the Prince criticises the two men who lead the families involved:

  'Three civil brawls, bred of an airy word,<br>
  By thee, old Capulet and Montague,<br>
  Have thrice disturbed the quiet of our streets'

- Use a / to show the line divide if it is less than two lines long.

  When Romeo first sets eyes on Juliet he is captivated by her; 'Her beauty hangs upon the cheek of night/Like a rich jewel in an Ethiops ear,' he whispers to himself.

One of the things that attracted specific criticism in previous assessment reports from examiners was the 'dumping' of quotations. Use them with finesse!

ISBN 9780170233293

# Examination success

## Preparing for examinations

Here are some things you can do to help revise for English examinations:

- Reread the texts you are using and think about them outside the English classroom – really knowing a text will make responding to a question much easier. (There is no merit in learning a class essay by rote to reproduce in the examination because the chances of getting the exact same question are remote).
- Put all your notes in order; go through them highlighting the important parts you want to remember.
- Check that you spell all names and titles exactly right.
- Rewrite essays to improve them – and practise writing to time – by hand. Students who type all their class assessments can find writing by hand for long periods in the examination difficult.
- Ask your teacher for appropriate tasks or questions on your texts.
- Check that you have all the handouts or references that have been provided for your class.
- Ask your teacher to mark your practice essays.
- And again – know your texts!

## Writing in the examinations

In examinations you are showing your knowledge, your responsiveness, and your ability to apply your knowledge appropriately. At Year 13 you are expected to be able to reveal independent thought and a personal response. And all this within a fixed time frame.

1 Apportion your time carefully.

   - Think more: write less – rambling on until you come to an answer is not a good use of time.
   - Think about the question, plan your response, then write your answer succinctly.

2 Follow instructions.

   - Read the question carefully. In 'close reading' the instructions are important:

     **In your own words** means do not quote from the text.

     **Identify and quote** means do give a label and a specific quotation. An overlong quotation will result in loss of marks.

     **Using specific evidence** means use quotation to support your idea – again not overlong.

     **Give one example** – if you give more than one, only the first will be considered.

- So, do not skim read a question – unpack it – highlight the key words; think first; do a small plan on the paper, it's yours; see if there are two (or more) parts to the question.
- This is also good advice for the essay questions – unpack the question first. Think about it, plan your response, then write your answer succinctly.


ISBN 9780170233293

3 Be familiar with basic terminology:

- **tense** does not mean tension
- **point of view** is not attitude
- **syntax** means sentence structure
- **poetic device** is not any old language feature
- **identify and quote** does not mean just quote
- **symbol** isn't mood
- **style** isn't content.

4 Write clearly.

- Handwriting must be legible – make it easy for your reader.
- Write in formal English.
- Avoid slang, especially teenage slang. Examiners hate 'sux'. So do we!
- Use punctuation properly.

5 Answer the question!

The following table summarises examiners' advice to you. Make sure that your work fits the right hand column. Help the examiner to enjoy marking your work!

| What examiners loathe | What examiners love |
|---|---|
| Illegible handwriting that's a struggle to read | Clear handwriting – that's easy to read |
| Teenage slang | Formal writing for a formal situation |
| Paragraphs of equal size that bear no relation to content | Paragraphs that are used to group ideas and are linked together |
| Proper nouns without capital letters | Proper nouns with capital letters |
| Incorrect spelling of names and key words, especially those copied from a text | Correct spelling of names and key words |
| A scattering of apostrophes | Apostrophes in their proper places |
| An introduction that doesn't introduce anything | An introduction that establishes where an essay is going |
| A weak conclusion that does not reach a satisfactory end | A strong conclusion that reaches a satisfactory reasoned end |
| A text used in the wrong category | A text used in the correct category |
| A question chosen that doesn't suit the text | A question chosen that suits the text |
| An essay that does not answer the question | An essay that answers the question |
| Students who regurgitate their class notes with no thought for the question | Students who think about their answer before they write and respond honestly to the question |
| Essays that just describe what happens | Essays that describe more than what happens – ie, ones that answer the question |
| Comments on the effect of words that show no awareness of the effect, like 'it sounds nice' and 'it emphasises' | Comments on the effect of words that say what the effect actually is |
| Students who quote from the text when the question says 'in your own words' | Students who do not quote from the text when the question says 'in your own words' |
| Students who cannot use terminology correctly | Students who know the meaning of technical terms and who use them correctly |
| Responses that do not answer the question | Responses that **ANSWER THE QUESTION** |

ISBN 9780170233293

## An aside on … Shakespeare

We notice that many schools have chosen not to teach Shakespeare. We hope yours is not one of them. You will find a chapter on responding critically to Shakespeare on our website www.cengage.co.nz/ach-eng-y13.

Yes, the language can be difficult at first, after all it is mainly in verse and does use old words; yes there are references to the Elizabethan age that you may not 'get'; yes, you may have to work hard with your teacher to understand fully what a play is about. It's worth the effort.

The stories Shakespeare tells are fascinating, all kinds of human experience are displayed and his characters are wonderfully complex and interesting. He has a brilliant turn of phrase; so brilliant that we still use many of his phrases hundreds of years later.

We speak English in New Zealand: we speak Shakespeare in New Zealand. Read the following, which explains what we mean. Essayist, drama critic and traveller, Bernard Levin, demonstrates Shakespeare's impact on our language:

> If you cannot understand my argument, and declare "It's Greek to me", you are quoting Shakespeare; if you claim to be more sinned against than sinning, you are quoting Shakespeare; if you recall your salad days, you are quoting Shakespeare; if you act more in sorrow than in anger, if your wish is father to the thought, if your lost property has vanished into thin air, you are quoting Shakespeare; if you have ever refused to budge an inch or suffered from green-eyed jealousy, if you have played fast and loose, if you have been tongue-tied, a tower of strength, hoodwinked or in a pickle, if you have knitted your brows, made a virtue of necessity, insisted on fair play, slept not one wink, stood on ceremony, danced attendance (on your lord and master), laughed yourself into stitches, had short shrift, cold comfort or too much of a good thing, if you have seen better days or lived in a fool's paradise - why, be that as it may, the more fool you, for it is a foregone conclusion that you are (as good luck would have it) quoting Shakespeare; if you think it is early days and clear out bag and baggage, if you think it is high time and that that is the long and short of it, if you believe that the game is up and that truth will out even if it involves your own flesh and blood, if you lie low till the crack of doom because you suspect foul play, if you have your teeth set on edge (at one fell swoop) without rhyme or reason, then - to give the devil his due - if the truth were known (for surely you have a tongue in your head) you are quoting Shakespeare; even if you bid me good riddance and send me packing, if you wish I were dead as a door-nail, if you think I am an eyesore, a laughing stock, the devil incarnate, a stony-hearted villain, bloody-minded or a blinking idiot, then - by Jove! O Lord! Tut, tut! for goodness' sake! what the dickens! but me no buts - it is all one to me, for you are quoting Shakespeare. (The Story of English, 145)

The RSA* says of Shakespeare: 'His output was prodigious, and his plays contain the whole range of human emotions, relationships, and situations. The themes are universal, encompassing every aspect of human endeavour. His language, rich in its imagery and dramatic power, moves fluently from heroic verse and lyricism to the broad humour of the street. His plays are read and performed in many languages** and have been turned into ballets, operas, music scores, films and cartoons. Moreover the acting of Shakespearean pieces by pupils*** is a means of exploring text and is a valid teaching approach. Seeing professional actors perform Shakespeare could also inspire curiosity and further study.'

* *Royal Society for the Encouragement of Arts, Manufactures and Commerce*
** *including Māori*
*** *congratulations to those involved in the Sheilah Wynn Shakespeare Festival*


ISBN 9780170233293

10

# Oral Presentations

Speaking in public has been identified as one of the major human fears, but the ability to make a speech is often the deciding factor in a person's success. That's why you are required to make speeches at school: to get ready for the outside world, where your ability to communicate clearly and coherently will be of huge benefit to you.

Like many fears, fear of public speaking is largely based on ignorance – ignorance of what makes a successful presentation and what is necessary to prepare for one. There are common factors in all successful spoken presentations. It is essential to be aware of these in order to confidently prepare and deliver a speech, debate, seminar or other speaking assignment.

*'All the great speakers were bad speakers at first.'*

*– Ralph Waldo Emerson*

As a student of Year 13 English you are likely to be involved in delivering an oral presentation. Although some students find this a most challenging thing to do, with the guidelines we have offered here, you will find speaking in front of an audience a little less daunting!

We have assumed you know what your topic will be and who will be in your audience. These factors will influence you. For example, if you are making your presentation to your classmates you might tailor some examples in your speech to their world; whereas if your speech is designed for the local council, comments about school might be completely inappropriate.

Here we offer general guidelines for preparation and delivery of speeches in general.

ISBN 9780170233293

**You will be expected to:**

- present a structured and carefully planned presentation
- develop ideas in a logical way using supporting material where appropriate
- be insightful and original
- integrate a range of oral techniques like variation in tone, volume, pace and emphasis, and visual ones too, like stance, gesture and body language
- reach the time limit set (approximately six minutes long, probably longer if group work or video clips are included)
- effectively facilitate group or class activities if you choose to incorporate them.

**Reading isn't speaking**

A student who reads his or her speech to the audience has not made a successful oral presentation. All the basics you have learnt about making a speech still apply. Advice like using cue cards, keep your chin up, move, make eye contact, modulate your voice, adjust your volume for the back row and so on. You know all this, you've been doing it – or trying to – for years!

You will need to work on adapting your information so that it is a more sophisticated, engaging and informative presentation at this level. It is an undeniable fact that a large percentage of your message is conveyed by methods other than just the spoken words. How you say these words and what the audience is seeing while you are saying them is also very important.

This section focuses on the techniques and skills you will need to deliver a successful presentation and achieve to your full potential. It will take practice. Read through the next section carefully and apply the advice to your presentation.

## Plan your attack

Think about the following things.

**What is the purpose of your presentation?**

- Why are you giving a presentation? To explain, to convince, to entertain? The purpose of your presentation will affect how you decide to structure it, what information you will include, the type of visual aids you may wish to use, etc.

**Who is your audience?**

In most cases this is likely to be your classmates and your teacher. Think about the following:

- What will they know about your subject?
- What background information do you need to provide?
- What technical terms will you need to explain and what can you assume they already know?
- How can you keep them interested?



ISBN 9780170233293

### What is the assessment schedule?

Ensure you have read through the assessment schedule carefully. Highlight the differences between reaching various levels and ensure you apply these to your presentation. It is important to keep referring back to the criteria throughout the planning and preparation process.

## Structure your material

In the same way that you structure a formal essay with care, it will be important for you to structure your presentation clearly for maximum effect. As a starting point, go back to what you know. Remind yourself about the structural elements your presentation will need to follow.

### Introduction

- Introduce your talk with a brief overview of the points you will cover.
- A good opening is sharp, snappy and to the point.
- Try to begin with an attention grabber to capture your audience's interest. Here are a few suggestions of ways to achieve a strong, attention-grabbing opening:

**1 Shock your listeners – make a startling opening statement**

You can be as startling as the situation will allow – as long as it has some link with the subject! You could begin with an interesting statistic, even including some audience involvement with this technique. For example a student making a speech about the film *Once Were Warriors* asked one quarter of the audience to stand and then said:

*'Statistics show that this is how many people in this room will have been exposed to domestic violence in their childhood.'*

**2 Arouse audience curiosity**

As a speaker you can whet your audience's appetite by a promise of valuable or interesting information to come.

*'By the time I finish speaking today, you will know all you need to know about …'*

**3 Ask a question**

This technique virtually forces the audience to give you their attention – because a relevant question is going to have every person in the room trying to answer it in their own minds. Questions should be relatively simple and easy to answer. The last thing you want is for the audience to still be thinking about their answer halfway through your speech.

*'Why do you text message more often than your Mum?'*

**4 Use 'special effects'**

Visual aids or effects can work well at the beginning of your speech. You might like to put a provoking image or quotation on a PowerPoint slide or on the white/blackboard, in order to gain the audience's attention and therefore focus them before you begin. Some students are more comfortable than others with using their voice and gestures together to focus attention on themselves. Make sure you are comfortable with an attention-grabbing device you choose to use!

ISBN 9780170233293

### The body

- Group your ideas into a logical order. Your speech needs to progress from introduction to conclusion.
- Keep focused on what is important, and ensure key ideas stand out. Repetition has its place in public speaking because the audience cannot rewind or re-read your points.
- Keep relevant and to the point. This is where planning a structured speech is so important. Those who ad lib tend to lose direction and finish up with a lot of ums and ers.
- Provide necessary evidence and examples. If you make a statement you should have at least one piece of evidence and/or an example to support that point.

### Conclusion

Simply because it is the last thing they will hear, an audience is likely to remember the conclusion more than any other part of the presentation. Therefore it is important that this part of the speech reinforces the main message.

Remember, the conclusion is not the place to introduce new information. It should, instead, be a concise summary of the information in the body of the speech.

In the same way that you seek to attract your audience's attention at the beginning of your presentation, so should you try to end in a dramatic, dynamic or positive way.


ISBN 9780170233293

## Planning a speech

Use the following chart to help plan your speech.

**TOPIC / ISSUE / FOCUS OF YOUR PRESENTATION:**

**INTRODUCTION:**

**BODY:**

What will be your main points? What evidence and examples will you add to support your points? How will you link the various points together in your presentation to draw conclusions and make judgements?

**FIRST POINT:**

**SUPPORTED BY:**

| Examples | Explanations |
| --- | --- |
| • | • |
| • | • |
| • | • |

ISBN 9780170233293

**OBSERVATIONS AND JUDGEMENTS DRAWN FROM THE FIRST POINT:**

- 
- 

**SECOND POINT:**

**SUPPORTED BY:**

Examples

- 
- 
- 

Explanations

- 
- 
- 

**THIRD POINT:**

**SUPPORTED BY:**

Examples

- 
- 
- 

Explanations

- 
- 
- 



ISBN 9780170233293

**FOURTH POINT:**

**SUPPORTED BY:**

Examples

-
-
-

Explanations

-
-
-

**CONCLUSION:**

**What points will you make in summary?**

Summary of findings/final observations/closure:

-
-
-

## Why do we have to do this?

Employers rate communication skills highly in their staff. When you go to work you will be using the skills in speaking and writing that you learnt at school. If you don't believe us, read the article on the next page.

ISBN 9780170233293

# Say it like you mean it

**By Julie Middleton.**

Afraid of standing up and speaking in public? You suffer from glossophobia - the fear of speech, or more to the point, having to deliver one in public. And you are not alone.

"Research tells me, and every book I've read tells me, that humans are more afraid of public speaking than dying," says Auckland actress and executive trainer Maggie Eyre. "We would rather be in the coffin than give the eulogy at the funeral."

But you can get over your fear, with a little help from Eyre's first book, *Speak Easy: the essential guide to speaking in public*.

In a chatty, non-technical book, the Encore Communications account director covers everything from finding your voice to posture and rehearsing, as well as specialist speeches for functions such as weddings, funerals and colleagues' farewells.

Eyre, who has a good number of New Zealand chief executives on her books, knows how you feel when you have to face a gaggle of expectant people.

Despite her evident confidence, she admits that public speaking once scared her stiff and can still make her nervous. But becoming a prefect at school in her teens made her realise "that speaking confidently in front of an assembly and class was part of the leadership role".

You just have to deal with it.

A lot of the fear rests in "our own negative belief systems. It has an impact on how you speak and how you project yourself. We're afraid of judgment, of looking silly in business when we have a responsibility to the business culture or the brand or the organisation."

That fear obscures a fact that many never consider.

"The audience never wants to see you fail, because if you fail, they feel embarrassed," says Eyre.

The solution is to fake it till you make it. "Project confidence, even if you don't feel it inside," says Eyre. "Over the years I've learned to act as if I'm confident although I might be shaking in my boots. After a while, you start to feel you are the confident person you're pretending to be."

The "fake it" mantra is one of 10 key tips the book outlines. Here are the other nine:

Believe in yourself. "The audience will believe you if you show them you're confident and comfortable in front of them," says Eyre. "Be positive. Use positive self-talk - 'my audience wants to listen to me and I am relaxed and confident, I know my material'."

Share true stories. "Don't play it safe - empower your audience, stimulate change in the mind of your listener," says Eyre. "Tell your own personal and professional story.

"Be yourself, be anecdotal, tell stories and be real. Sure, you've got to toe the business line, but involve yourself."

Plan and prepare well. "Procrastination is a killer. Take time to do the necessary research before writing your speech.

"Do a little every day, even if it's just jotting down a few notes. Leaving preparation until the last minute will make you stressed and the speech won't be as good.

"Winston Churchill estimated it took him six to eight hours to prepare a 45-minute speech. Serious speakers need at least 45 to 60 minutes of preparation time per minute of speaking."

Know your key messages. "What do you want audiences to remember from your speech? Write them down and memorise them. You can then weave these key messages into your storytelling"

Rehearse in front of a colleague or friend. "Have a complete run-through," says Eyre. "A rehearsal is vital for your self-confidence ... sports teams practise before the big day. It's very simple - if you don't rehearse ... you won't have had the opportunity to discover any unexpected problems."

Warm up before speaking. Stand up, with feet shoulder-width apart, and breathe deeply, Eyre says. Do some bending and stretching, some star jumps. Movement gets more feel-good endorphins to the brain.

And, yes, warm up your voice and jaw, just like an actor or singer. Repeat phrases such as "unique New York" or "red leather, yellow leather" or blow raspberries.

Seek out and accept training "Don't wait for a really important speech to practise your public speaking. Presentation skills courses abound - make the most of them."

Be well-informed and read the paper every day. This will expand your knowledge and vocabulary.

Find a mentor. "Everyone needs someone to believe in their talent."

...

The number one Kiwi speech impediment, says Eyre, is lack of preparation, closely followed by reading a speech from behind the lectern and keeping your eyes down. "Eye contact is really important."

Number three is having all the text of a speech on screen behind the speaker, "so there's no room for engagement between you and the audience".

Fourth is the classic New Zealand rising intonation at the end of sentences, which makes them sound like questions.

So is it necessary to make people laugh when giving a speech?

"I tell clients not to tell jokes because inevitably you will offend somebody," cautions Eyre.

"I think it's great to make people laugh, but send yourself up - be careful about other people. I've had people make fun of me when they've been making speeches and I have not appreciated it. You don't know what people's sensitive points are.

"My best humour is when I don't plan it - say, when I make a mistake."



ISBN 9780170233293

# Presentation techniques

Many speakers spend most of their preparation time working on the words alone. This means that the other components that contribute so much to their message (or detract from it) – their use of their voice and body language – mostly happen by accident.

## Integrating presentation techniques

The basic idea behind an oral presentation is to deliver a range of material on a certain subject in a dynamic and interesting way that ensures your audience is engaged and learning. Your task is to ensure your audience is involved in your presentation (this makes it easier for you to present well and them to listen well), remembering of course that the techniques you use are not supposed to dominate the presentation; the fundamental aim is to impart information!

There are important decisions for you to make about how you will present your key ideas. Let's have a look at some of the common techniques.

### Visual aids

Six minutes is a long time for anyone (particularly teenagers!) to sit and listen to someone speaking, therefore it is important that you give them other things to focus on and help make your specific points clearly. Our 21st century culture is highly visual, so an effective way of helping your audience to listen well is to incorporate visual aids into your presentation. However, use of visual aids requires careful planning, because what can add greatly to a presentation may also distract from it.

#### PowerPoint

- When preparing PowerPoint and other multimedia programs, always aim for a simple, uncluttered look. Do not use too many varieties of background, font or animations.
- Be sure the machinery works, the screen is in place and clean, and that the light is satisfactory for seeing the display easily from all parts of the audience.
- Use a remote if possible to change the slides as it allows you to move away from the keyboard. If you must use a keyboard, have it at lectern height so that you can remain upright. Another way is to have a helper move the slides on for you.
- Stand facing the audience and glance at the computer screen in front of you, not behind you to the projected image.
- Don't read out words written on the slide. Assume your audience can read them for themselves. Pause to allow this to happen if there are lots of words to read on any one slide.
- Make sure the first and last slides support your introduction and conclusion respectively.

#### Whiteboard

- Unless you are a confident, quick writer you will need to spend time putting your information onto the whiteboard before you begin.
- Leave any underlining, circling of key words, etc, to do through your presentation so there are points of contact or focus for the audience.
- Do not stand and write anything more than a few words or lines that will mean your back is to the audience for any more than a couple of seconds.

ISBN 9780170233293

## YouTube (or DVD) clips

- These may create a successful attention-grabbing opening or may act as interesting punctuation for your speech.
- You will not be able to include the entirety of a video clip as part of your six minutes. Negotiate with your teacher to ensure you reach the required length for the spoken part of your presentation.

## Photocopied material

- A handout must be available for every person in your audience, so work out the cost before deciding to use one.
- You must refer to the handout in your speech. Don't just pass it out and forget about it.
- Handouts can provide pictures, statistics, examples, even activities for your audience. But beware the distraction they can also create. Watch what happens in a classroom when a teacher gives out a handout …
- Some ideas for handouts might be:
  - With a factual handout you might get students to highlight certain points as you go through.
  - You might leave empty boxes, lines, etc, for students to fill in as they listen to your speech and/or watch your PowerPoint.

## Posters

- A poster may help to focus the interest of your audience and settle them in the moments before you begin speaking.
- If you are going to refer to a poster, it will need to be big enough for people to see the detail clearly. Some ideas may include: a map of an area, picture of author for 'recognition', covers of books, film posters, etc.

### There are several overriding rules when using visual aids:

- Your visual aid will not be effective if it is merely put up or switched on and left in the background. You should be prepared to refer to important visual points as you speak to your audience as this will integrate the resource into your presentation. Practising how you will highlight key points displayed for your audience, talking to those points and integrating the resource(s) into your presentation is an important preparation.
- Whatever visual aid you choose to use, you will need to practise using these resources in order to integrate the material successfully.
- If you practise you will know where your visual aids will fit in with your text, that you won't be shuffling around in a heap of notes and that you will not 'dry up'. Also, most importantly, you'll get the timing right.
- Keeping visual aids clear, simple and uncluttered will ensure that they impact on your audience, rather than confuse them.
- Check with your teacher that the techniques and resources you plan to use in various parts of your presentation are suitable and appropriate for your purpose.

  And finally …
- Know how to turn your equipment on and off!


ISBN 9780170233293

## Involving your audience: using group techniques

If you are already a confident speaker, you may like to experiment with some more sophisticated techniques. A successful presentation may include involving your audience in some way – after all six minutes is a long time! It is a good idea to give your audience a break from listening and give them a task to do.

For example you might choose to involve your audience in a 'question and answer' situation. In order for this to be effective, it will require careful preparation. You could present your audience with some brief activity (for example, a short significant quotation from your text) and lead a brief 'question and answer session' based on the quotation. *'Raise your hand if you like this metaphor.'* Alternatively, you might be talking about marketing: *'Stand up if you think this product is going to sell'.*

Another possibility is for you to set some kind of pair or group exercise and then lead the group discussion or feedback that arises from this work. Remember, your classmates are going to try and make this experience as easy as possible for you. Rely on their maturity but do your preparation to ensure that you can keep to time.

There are certain things to keep in mind when facilitating a group activity.

- Make sure your instructions are clear. You may like to have them on an OHT, PowerPoint slide or as part of your handout, so they can be referred back to.
- Think about how you will divide the class into groups. You do not want to waste time so pre-plan size/placement/division of groups.
- Work out very carefully how much time you will allow for the activity. You don't want it to take too long, nor do you want to rush them. Practising this with friends would be extremely useful.
- You will need to circulate around the room in order to check that groups are on task. It also gives your 'students' time to ask questions.
- Most importantly, you will need to make a clear connection between the task they have carried out and your presentation!

### Ideas for group work:

- Students can categorise types of words into certain groups.
- Students can analyse an advertisement according to your material (and feedback to class).

Teachers are experts at group facilitation, after all their job is to present to each class that comes through the door. Watch carefully how some teachers carry out group work successfully, in particular noting the instructions they give and how they gather the class' attention when the activity is finished.

### Remember the basics!

It is easy to focus on the tricky bits of oral presentation but effective visual aids are used only to support your spoken words; they cannot take the place of basic delivery skills!

ISBN 9780170233293

## Delivery

- Do not read from pages of notes. Use your visual aids for cues and have brief back-up notes on cards or light cardboard about A5 size or smaller. (Don't try to memorise your talk word-for-word and do not write it out word-for-word on your cue cards.)
- Use appropriate language, get the right level of formality/informality.
- If you think you are going to stumble over a particular word or phrase, use a different one if you can. Otherwise, rehearse it enough times so that it trips off the tongue. Some speakers recite tongue twisters before 'going on' to loosen up their voice. Try 'red leather, yellow leather' a few times or 'she sells sea shells by the sea shore'.
- Don't use too many 'fillers' – too many 'ums' and 'ahs' will irritate your audience.
- Practise in front of a mirror so that you can see your facial expression.
- Tape your speech and listen to yourself to check that your voice sounds normal, not monotonous. Work towards an appropriate tone, pace and volume.
- Sound and look enthusiastic. If you want your audience to be interested in your talk, then you must show interest and enthusiasm yourself.
- Pitch your voice at the back row, not the front row. To keep the attention of your audience they need to be able to hear you – though incorporating a whisper when sharing a 'secret' or shouting when emphasising a 'truth' can all be part of the performance.

## Body language

- Where will you stand in relation to the equipment you are using? If you are using a screen, make sure you don't stand in front of it.
- Try to adopt a relaxed posture but not so relaxed that you look sloppy or unprofessional. Stand on both feet.
- Avoid nervous gestures such as waving your hands around needlessly, clicking a pen, or brandishing a pointer.
- Make eye contact with your audience. Try to avoid gazing over people's heads or looking down at your notes too often. If you find it difficult to make eye contact, concentrate on a couple of friendly faces for a few seconds at a time.

### Practice makes perfect

Being prepared means rehearsing your presentation as many times as it takes to get it right. This will increase your confidence and allow you to feel more relaxed and sure that everything will work on the day. As we have already said it is important that you choose your delivery techniques carefully and practise everything. Your friends and family make perfect test audiences and can give you ideas on where you need to practise more or how you could improve your presentation.



ISBN 9780170233293

## What goes where?

You spend plenty of time planning and writing your speech, and its content is of great importance. However, because this is specifically an oral presentation you are assessed as much on the delivery of your speech as its content. So far in this chapter we have dealt with these two components separately, but you need to integrate them effectively if you are to be rewarded for your efforts. You should probably spend as much time planning the presentation techniques you will use and where you will use them, as you spend assembling the information you will use.

Before you actually deliver your speech you need to:

1 Photocopy/print out your speech twice. If it is on a computer leave wide margins (at least 6cm) to allow annotation and note-taking.

2 Head the first copy 'Body Language/ Movement'. Read through your speech identifying (by highlighting and annotating) where it would be appropriate to use:

- gesture for added interest
- gesture for emphasis
- facial expression to match words
- movement
- eye contact for emphasis
- visual aids.

3 Head the second copy 'Voice'. Go through the same process but this time highlight and annotate where it would be appropriate to use:

- intonation for reinforcement
- pause for effect and/or emphasis
- an area to speak – slowly/ quickly/loudly
- breath – you may like to use a pencil to mark a / wherever you are going to take a breath.

4 Spend time practising your speech from each of the copies. Once you are confident with both, begin to join the two together.

5 Write your speech onto cue (or palm) cards. Using a highlighter or alternate coloured pen, mark the places you will use various techniques, for example:

- a forward slash ( / ) for a breath
- underlining ( __ ) for emphasis
- highlighting single words where you will change your tone
- an asterisk ( * ) for a gesture.

6 Rehearse! The worst crime for a speechmaker is to read his or her speech. You cannot possibly hope to present your ideas with confidence and use delivery techniques in a sustained way unless you know your speech well. Remember … spend time getting confident with your speech. Ironically enough, it will help you develop 'spontaneity'!

ISBN 9780170233293

# 11 Syntax (Sentence Structure)

Understanding sentence structure helps you to appreciate the way writers write. You will remember most of this from previous study, but let's just recap.

**Firstly a definition:**

**Syntax**

*Pronunciation*: /ˈsɪntaks/

*noun [mass noun]*

- **1** the arrangement of words and phrases to create well-formed sentences in a language: *the syntax of English*
- a set of rules for or an analysis of the syntax of a language: *generative syntax*
- the branch of linguistics that deals with syntax
- **2** the structure of statements in a computer language

*Origin*:

late 16th century: from French *syntaxe*, or via late Latin from Greek *suntaxis*, from *sun* 'together' + *tassein* 'arrange'

*Grammar*:

The study of how words are selected and arranged to form sentences. Syntax is a major part of grammar, the other being morphology.

*from* ***Oxford Dictionaries online***

**Secondly some reminders:**

## 1 Sentences and complete sentences

**Q** **What is a sentence?**

You will already know this basic definition.

**A** A group of words, beginning with a capital letter and ending with a full stop, that makes complete sense by itself.



ISBN 9780170233293

For example: i The First XI cricket team played well yesterday.
ii The captain was happy with his team.

**Q** **What is a complete sentence?**

**A** A complete sentence is a group of words containing a subject and a finite verb.

**This creates more questions:**

**Q** **What is a subject?**

**A** A subject is what or who is performing the action or being the state referred to by the verb.

For example: i *The First XI cricket team* played well yesterday.
ii *The captain* was happy with his team.

**Q** **What is a finite verb?**

**A** A verb is often defined as a 'doing word'. However, this definition is not enough for our purposes. The following examples all fit the 'doing word' definition but they are not finite, they do not indicate when the action happened.

For example: *To go* (infinitive)
*To go* onto the field.

This is not a complete sentence because it lacks a subject and the verb is not finite. A complete sentence might be created by adding the auxiliary verb *had.*

The fielders *had to go* onto the field.

For example: *going* (present participle)
*Going* onto the field.

This is not a complete sentence because it lacks a subject and the verb is not finite – it does not say when this happened. A complete sentence might be created by adding the auxiliary verb *will be.*

The batsmen *will be going* onto the field.

For example: *gone* (past participle)
'Bowling gone well?'

This is not a complete sentence because the verb is not finite. A complete sentence might be created by adding the auxiliary verb *has.*

'*Has* the bowling gone well?'

(However, note that in speech this sentence fragment would be perfectly acceptable. The rules are often broken!)

ISBN 9780170233293

**So back to the original question ...**

**Q** **What is a finite verb?**

**A** A complete or **finite** verb is one that links to the subject and places the action or state in a time (past? present? future?).

For example: *played* (what the team did and when – in the past)
*was* (the captain's state and when – in the past).

Identify, by underlining and labelling, the subject and verb in the following sentences:

i The batsmen scored 150 runs.

ii The wicket keeper took four catches.

## 2 Minor sentences

**Q** **What is a minor sentence?**

**A** A minor sentence is one without a finite verb or without a subject, but punctuated as if it is complete.

For example: **i** *White figures on a green landscape.*
**ii** *Racing between the wickets.*

In the first example you can see the subject but there is no verb to tell you what these white figures are doing. In the second example there is no subject – who is racing? – and only the present participle is given so we cannot tell if this is in the past, present or future.

Rewrite sentences i and ii above so they are complete.

i ______________________________

ii ______________________________



ISBN 9780170233293

## 3 More basic terms to understand

Main clause
Subordinate clause
Phrase (adverbial and adjectival)
Simple sentence
Compound sentence
Complex sentence
Compound-complex sentence

**Q** **What is a clause?**

**A** A clause is a group of words containing a finite verb that is part of a longer sentence.

For example: The bowler bowled a bouncer and the batsman ducked.

This sentence has two main clauses: *The bowler bowled a bouncer* *the batsman ducked.*

Each clause could be a separate complete simple sentence (each has a subject and one finite verb), but the two clauses of equal importance are joined by a conjunction (and). This type of sentence is called a **compound sentence.**

Identify the two main clauses in this sentence:

The two umpires left the pitch and the rain began to fall.

(YOBFANS is a mnemonic to remind you that in strict grammatical terms the only conjunctions that can be used to join compound sentences are: yet, of, but, for, and, nor, so.)

**Q** **What is a subordinate clause?**

**A** A subordinate clause is a group of words with a finite verb, which need to be attached to other parts of the sentence to make sense.

For example: *After the umpire spoke to the captains ...*

There is a subject and a finite verb but the use of the word *After* means that this clause needs to be linked to another before the sentence makes complete sense.

For example: *After the umpire spoke to the captains, the two teams retired to the dressing rooms.*

This type of sentence with one main clause and at least one subordinate clause is called a complex sentence. It is possible to add more clauses to sentences.

For example: *After the umpire spoke to the captains, the two teams retired to the dressing rooms and they waited for the rain to stop.*

ISBN 9780170233293

This sentence with two main and at least one subordinate clause is called a compound-complex sentence.

Identify the clauses in this sentence:

When the rain stopped the two teams came out onto the field and play resumed.

NB: A semi-colon can be used to suggest a connection between two clauses, drawing attention to the latter clause.

For example: *The umpire raised his arm; the batsman was out.*

**Q What is a phrase?**

**A** A phrase is a group of words forming part of a sentence without a finite verb. Some specifically relate to when or where or how something is happening and so are called adverbial phrases.

For example: *While speaking to the fielder …*
*Earlier that afternoon …*
*… as quickly as he could.*

Some specifically relate to a person, place or thing mentioned in the sentence and are therefore called adjectival phrases.

For example: *Wearing a battered green cap …*
*Using colourful, crude language to express his disappointment …*

If you can grasp these basic ideas and have them at your disposal as you analyse pieces of writing, you will be able to express your ideas more expertly with correct terminology.

However, we do stress that this is the tip of a very big iceberg and there are places to go to for more information. Look in the library, or on the Internet if this kind of analysis interests you!



ISBN 9780170233293

# Coping with syntax

If you were asked to comment on the syntax of a passage, how would you cope? To help identify the syntax:

- You can separate the sentences.
- You can use brackets and/or different coloured highlighters to identify the clauses and/or phrases in the sentence. Look for completed verbs.

But this exercise doesn't often help you to understand why each sentence has been composed in a certain way. You have to think about the *effect* of that sentence on the way information is being presented. And you need to think about that sentence in relation to the others around it. For example, a short simple sentence after a long complicated one is often there for effect – perhaps to draw the reader's attention to what is said in the short sentence.

## Examples of sentence structure

Most sentences in English start with the main point (main clause) and go on to add other ideas to it. These sentences are called **loosely coordinated** ones. For example:

> *The white stone hotel was set high on the cliff top, from where it looked down onto the blue sea and the island out in the gulf.*

Here the subject is introduced immediately (the hotel) in the main clause and its surroundings are added in a subordinate clause. This structure is the one most closely resembling normal speech.

A sentence written with the subject at the end, like this ...

> *Set high on the cliff, from where it looked down onto the blue sea and the island out in the gulf, was the white stone hotel.*

... is called a **periodic** sentence. The reader has to wait to know what he/she is reading about. Such sentences are often used to create suspense.

Another structure is the **balanced** sentence where two ideas are balanced against each other:

> *The hotel was the perfect place for a holiday; it was also the perfect place for a wedding.*

If the two ideas are contrasting then it is an **antithetical** sentence:

> *The hotel was the perfect place for a wedding; it was the worst place for a divorce.*

ISBN 9780170233293

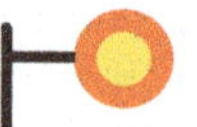

## Syntax in action

Let's look at the structure of a piece of professional writing. The following passage is taken from a novel titled *The Book and the Brotherhood* by Iris Murdoch. The author is describing the aftermath of a university summer ball.

The passage is presented as a complete paragraph. Read it through more than once to get an idea of its content.

It was now full daylight, the terrible inquisitional finalising daylight had come, sending away the enchanted forest and all the magic of the night and revealing a scene, more resembling a battlefield, of trampled grass, empty bottles, broken glasses, upturned chairs, errant garments, and every sort of unattractive human debris. Even the tents, in the relentless sunshine, looked dirty and bedraggled. The blackbirds, thrushes, tits, swallows, wrens, robins, starlings and innumerable other birds were singing loudly, the doves were cooing and the rooks were cawing, and, nearer now, in the big trees of the deer park, came the hollow repetitive cry of the cuckoo. Dance music continued unabated however, sounding in the more open space of the high cloudless blue sky and surrounded by all that bird song, diminished and unreal. A queue was forming for breakfast, but a considerable number of people seemed unable to stop dancing, possessed by ecstasy or by a frenzied desire to maintain the enchantment, and to postpone the misery to come: remorse, regret, the tarnished hope, the shattered dream, and all the awful troubles of ordinary life. Gull would have liked some breakfast, the idea of bacon and eggs was suddenly extremely attractive, but he did not fancy waiting in the queue by himself, and he felt a more urgent and immediate need to sit down, preferably to lie down. He decided to rest for a short time and to come for the grub later when the crush was less.

Here is the same passage rewritten in its separate sentences for you to see if you can identify its clauses and phrases and discover if the sentences are mainly loosely coordinated ones.

Use a highlighter to identify the completed verbs, the main clauses, the dependent clauses, the phrases and the sentence types.



ISBN 9780170233293

It was now full daylight, the terrible inquisitional finalising daylight had come, sending away the enchanted forest and all the magic of the night and revealing a scene, more resembling a battlefield, of trampled grass, empty bottles, broken glasses, upturned chairs, errant garments, and every sort of unattractive human debris.

Even the tents, in the relentless sunshine, looked dirty and bedraggled.

The blackbirds, thrushes, tits, swallows, wrens, robins, starlings and innumerable other birds were singing loudly, the doves were cooing and the rooks were cawing, and, nearer now, in the big trees of the deer park, came the hollow repetitive cry of the cuckoo.

Dance music continued unabated however, sounding in the more open space of the high cloudless blue sky and surrounded by all that bird song, diminished and unreal.

A queue was forming for breakfast, but a considerable number of people seemed unable to stop dancing, possessed by ecstasy or by a frenzied desire to maintain the enchantment, and to postpone the misery to come: remorse, regret, the tarnished hope, the shattered dream, and all the awful troubles of ordinary life.

Gull would have liked some breakfast, the idea of bacon and eggs was suddenly extremely attractive, but he did not fancy waiting in the queue by himself, and he felt a more urgent and immediate need to sit down, preferably to lie down.

He decided to rest for a short time and to come for the grub later when the crush was less.

ISBN 9780170233293

## Answering questions on syntax

For some students this analysis is an interesting exercise (for others it is not!) – but, for all of us, the purpose in identifying the sentence structure is to see how the writer has used it for effect.

1 How would you answer the question: 'Comment on the structure of the first sentence.'?

You might begin by breaking it down into its clauses and phrases.

| | |
|---|---|
| It was now full daylight, | *main clause* |
| the terrible inquisitional finalising daylight had come, | *main clause* |
| sending away the enchanted forest and all the magic of the night | *non-finite adverbial –ing dependent clause* |
| and revealing a scene, more resembling a battlefield, of trampled grass, empty bottles,broken glasses, upturned chairs, errant garments, and every sort of unattractive human debris. | *non-finite adverbial –ing dependent clause* |

Now look at what the writer is showing you in the opening description of the scene, how she builds up an image for you and links what you can see to what she wants you to think and feel about the scene. Use the space below to complete your answer.


ISBN 9780170233293

## Your answer might be something like this:

1 Comment on the structure of the first sentence.

This opening sentence is a loosely coordinated one (main clauses first with additional dependent clauses). The writer gives the basic fact that it is day at the very beginning 'It was now full daylight' in the first clause and then goes on to add three adjectives 'terrible, inquisitional, finalizing' in the second main clause to describe the effect the daylight has on the people who have been at the party. These words suggest that the aftermath will be unpleasant; that there will be unpleasant questions to be faced about what happened and that the good time is definitely over.

The two dependent clauses, which follow, continue these ideas. The first uses the enchanted forest metaphor to suggest that the party had been magical, a fairytale-like occasion but that daylight, as in all fairy tales, has brought back reality. The second dependent clause emphasises this reality by using the image of a battlefield and adding several phrases in a list effect: 'empty bottles, broken glasses, upturned chairs' to show the reader what the place actually looks like. The final phrase of this clause 'every sort of human debris' sums up the unpleasantness by using the word 'debris', a word that suggests broken, spoilt, unwanted things.

The overall effect of the whole sentence is reinforced by its structure, which leads the reader from a simple statement to a full emotional and visual appreciation of the scene.

## Using the previous question and answer as a model, answer the following:

2 Look carefully at sentence 3. The writer now moves from what is visible to what can be heard. Comment on the way the writer has used nouns and verbs in this sentence.

ISBN 9780170233293

3 Sentence 4 continues this focus on sound. What does it suggest?

4 Comment on the use of the main clause and the colon in sentence 5.

5 It is only at this stage in the paragraph that the writer introduces us to a character. What does sentence 6 tell us about Gull and why, do you think, is this sentence not at the beginning of the paragraph?



ISBN 9780170233293

**Compare your answers with the suggestions offered here. Go back and look at the passage again if you have missed out anything.**

2 Look carefully at sentence 3. The writer now moves from what is visible to what can be heard. Comment on the way the writer has used nouns and verbs in this sentence.

The majority of the nouns are names of birds: 'blackbirds ... robins ... rooks ... cuckoo' and the verbs are mostly the sounds that these birds are making: 'singing ... cooing ... cawing'. These are presented in a loosely coordinated sentence to emphasise for the reader the proliferation of natural sound and its infinite variety.

3 Sentence 4 continues this focus on sound. What does it suggest?

The sentence begins with the main clause, the main fact that the dance music was still playing. It goes on to add in successive dependent clauses that this music is less attractive by day than by night 'diminished and unreal'. This adds to the general unattractiveness of the scene.

4 Comment on the use of the main clause and the colon in sentence 5.

The sentence begins with two main clauses joined by the conjunction 'but'. The first clause shows that some people have moved on from the party and are beginning the next day by queuing for breakfast. The second clause tells that others have not moved on, and their now rather pathetic attempt to keep the party going and the reasons for their desire to do this are what informs the remainder of the sentence.

The colon is used to introduce a list of examples of the things in their lives to which the students at the ball who are still dancing at dawn are trying to avoid returning: 'remorse, regret, the tarnished hope'

The writer is suggesting that the 'enchantment' of the ball is no more than a 'shattered dream' and that real life is full of distress, 'and all the awful troubles of ordinary life'.

ISBN 9780170233293

5 It is only at this stage in the paragraph that the writer introduces us to a character. What does sentence 6 tell us about Gull and why, do you think, this sentence is not at the beginning of the paragraph?

Gull wants breakfast, he has had enough of the ball; but he is lonely, does not want to queue by himself and is not feeling too well, he needs to lie down.

The writer has set the scene in which Gull plays a part before introducing him. The reader can imagine the place, what it looks like, what it sounds like and how the people are behaving and, to some extent, feeling through the description of the atmosphere. This helps the reader to empathise with the character when the focus of the passage turns to him.

## A final word on syntax

We hope that by studying the way other writers use sentences to good effect, you will see ways to improve your own writing and create accurate, well-constructed sentences yourself.



ISBN 9780170233293

12

# Language Lists

As a senior student of English you must be able to identify features of language in the text you are studying, whether it be an extract or a complete work. However it is even more important that you are able to explain the effect or contribution these features make to things such as the impact, purpose, structure, theme or tone of the text you are studying.

In this section we are presenting you with a comprehensive list of terminology for you to check what you know, what you recognise but do not fully understand, and what is completely new to you. The techniques are grouped under useful sub-headings:

- Literary
- Grammar and syntax
- Figures of speech
- Parts of speech
- Poetic devices
- Visual
- Film
- Oral

Please note that some terms are not restricted to one grouping. For example, we have listed 'antithesis' and 'tricolon' under Oral because students often meet them when studying speeches. You may also need to use them when close reading a novel, newspaper article or magazine column.

Think about the technical terms that you need to use when you write answers in chemistry – you need similarly precise language to comment successfully on English texts and this list will help you to add depth and detail to your answers.

You will notice that in the left-hand margin there are three circles labelled – 'I know', 'I need to check' and 'I have no idea!' Read through the list and tick the box that best describes your knowledge of each literary term. Use this chapter to increase your personal word bank of literary terminology. By the end of the year we hope every 'I know' box is ticked.

I know | I need to check | I have no idea

## Literary

○ ○ ○ **Allegory**
A story or situation written in such a way as to have two coherent meanings. Example: Orwell's *Animal Farm*

○ ○ ○ **Anti-hero**
A protagonist lacking the usual qualities associated with heroes.

○ ○ ○ **Antithesis**
Placing contrasting terms or ideas close together to emphasise their difference and give the effect of balance.
Example: For fools rush in where angels fear to tread.

○ ○ ○ **Apostrophe**
A direct address to a person or personified idea.
Example: *O Romeo, Romeo, wherefore art thou Romeo?*

○ ○ ○ **Archaism**
A word or expression not quite obsolete but no longer in current use.

ISBN 9780170233293

I know | I need to check | I have no idea

○○○ **Aside**
A dramatic convention in which a participant in the action directly addresses the audience; other characters on the stage are not supposed to hear the aside.

○○○ **Ballad**
A poem or song (which tells a story) in simple, colloquial language.

○○○ **Climax**
The effect of adding one word or phrase to another with increasing importance or impressiveness. It also means 'a series of incidents which rise in dramatic intensity to reach a crisis which is then resolved'.

○○○ **Comedy**
'Comedy' is used most often with reference to a kind of drama which is intended primarily to entertain the audience, and which ends happily for the characters.

○○○ **Dramatic monologue**
A passage in which a single person, not the writer, is speaking.

○○○ **Elegy**
A poem lamenting a person's death eg. Tennyson's *In Memoriam.*

○○○ **Epic**
A long, narrative poem in elevated style about the exploits of superhuman heroes.

○○○ **Genre**
A particular type of text that has distinctive characteristics.
Examples: thriller, romance, science fiction.

○○○ **Irony**
A figure of speech in which the point intended is different from (usually the opposite of) the literal meaning of the words used. Whenever irony is concerned there are two attitudes to the subject: a surface attitude and an underlying attitude.
There are several types of irony:
1. Dramatic irony: occurs when the audience is aware of factors affecting a character that the character is unaware of.
2. Socratic irony: pretending to adopt someone else's viewpoint in order to ridicule them or their ideas.
3. Sarcasm: strong and obvious disapproval given as pretended praise (eg. Hitler was a nice guy)
4. Understatement (or meiosis): here the true magnitude of something is minimised eg. It is sometimes a bit cold at the North Pole.
5. Verbal irony: a figure of speech where the point intended is different from, and usually the opposite (antithesis) of the literal meaning of the words.

I know | I need to check | I have no idea

○○○ **Light verse**
Poetry that deals with trivial matters or adopts a light-hearted approach to a grave subject.

○○○ **Lyric poetry**
Typically, this is a short poem where the poet expresses personal feelings, usually about love.

○○○ **Metonymy**
The substitution of one word for another closely associated with it. eg. The crown will find an heir.

○○○ **Narrative verse**
Poetry that tells a story.

○○○ **Ode**
A long lyric poem with intricate stanza forms, seriousness of purpose and grandeur of style.

○○○ **Oxymoron**
Two words or phrases or opposite or contrasting meaning placed together for effect.
Example: Parting is such sweet sorrow.

○○○ **Parody**
An imitation of a specific work of literature devised so as to ridicule its characteristic features.

○○○ **Protagonist**
The person the story is about.

I know | I need to check | I have no idea

○○○ **Revenge tragedy**
A special form of tragedy which concentrates on the protagonist's pursuit of vengeance against those who have done him wrong eg. *Hamlet*.

○○○ **Satire**
Literature which exhibits or examines vice and folly and makes them appear ridiculous or contemptible.

○○○ **Soliloquy**
A monologue spoken by the characters on the stage; usually it either indicates what is to happen later in the play or expresses the innermost thoughts of the speaker.

○○○ **Sonnet**
A lyric poem of fixed form: 14 lines of iambic pentameter, rhymed and organised according to several intricate schemes. In general the ideas developed in a sonnet accord loosely with these divisions, which are marked by rhyme.

○○○ **Tragedy**
A play that traces the career and downfall of an individual, and shows in their downfall both the capacities and limitations of human life.

## Grammar and syntax

○○○ **Apostrophe (')**
Has two main purposes: the first to show ownership; the second to show omitted letters within a contraction.
Example: My friend's father offered to pay for me, which wasn't a good idea at all.

○○○ **Brackets ( )**
Most commonly used to include extra information within a sentence.
Example: She said to me (for the millionth time), 'Go on, have a go.'



ISBN 9780170233293

I know | I need to check | I have no idea

### Clause
A group of words containing a finite verb (ie. a verb with a subject) in a sentence of two or more finite verbs. If there is only one finite verb in a sentence we call it a simple sentence. A main clause is an independent one, but a sub-ordinate clause is dependent (on a main clause).

### Colon (:)
Introduces more information or shows divisions.
Example: I have lots of reasons: I'm too scared, I'm too poor, I'm not interested, the rope might break, I value my life!

### Comma (,)
Tells the reader when to take a short pause in a sentence.
Example: I was supposed to do a bungy jump, but then I decided I was too scared.

### Complex sentence
One main clause joined to one or more subordinate clauses. A writer uses a complex sentence to express an idea that requires more elaboration.
Example: The student asked a question when he had a problem with his classwork.

### Compound sentence
Two or more main clauses (simple sentences) joined together with a conjunction or separated by a semi-colon. A compound sentence gives us more information than a simple sentence by developing a basic idea.
Example: The student asked a question and the teacher answered it.

### Compound-complex sentence
Two or more main clauses linked to one or more subordinate clauses.
Example: The student asked a question and the teacher answered it because the teacher knew the student needed help.

### Contraction
A word shortened in speech or spelling eg. He would've.

### Dash (–)
Has three main purposes: the first to indicate a sudden change of thought; the second to lead to the unexpected; the third to give extra information.
Example: I couldn't get out of it – but wait – maybe there was another way.

### Demonstratives
Words such as 'this', 'that', 'these' followed by a noun, as in 'this book'.

### Exclamation mark (!)
Used at the end of a sentence that shows strong feeling.
Example: 'I would never do something so stupid!'

### Hyphens (-)
Used to join two or more words to make a compound word and to divide words at the end of a line.
Example: I looked straight into the eyes of my so-called best friend.

### Inverted commas (")
Inverted commas (speech marks) are used to show the words being said by a speaker. Only the actual words spoken go inside the speech marks.
Example: 'OK, I'll do it, but only if you come with me – in tandem!' 'You're on!' she whooped. 'Let's go!'

### Minor sentence
A sentence without a completed verb that is often used for emphasis. Many common greetings are also minor sentences. Minor sentences are frequently used in advertising as they give a passage an informal, casual, clipped, fast tone. They also emphasise key words within the sentence.
Example: (1) Hello. (2) Never in a million years.

### Paradox
This is a statement whose parts seem mutually contradictory, yet which make sense after deeper consideration.
Example: Deep down he's really shallow.

### Question mark (?)
Used at the end of a sentence (or clause) that asks a direct question.

### Semi-colon (;)
Used to break up long sentences and lists or join clauses that are closely related.
Example: My close friend told me I should try it; but she wasn't going to do it herself.

### Simple sentence
A group of words, including a verb, that makes sense on its own. Simple sentences are commonly used to describe a single idea.
Example: The student asked a question.

## Figures of speech

### Allusion
A reference to something related indirectly to the subject matter of prose or poetry. Example: 'I am tied to the stake, and I must stand the course.' An allusion to bear-baiting *(King Lear)*.

### Coinage
The making of new words for a special purpose: much favoured in advertising.
Example: Donut (doughnut), Schweppervescence etc.

### Extended metaphor
The comparison between two things is continued beyond the first point of comparison. This technique extends and deepens a description.
Example:
How long have they tugged the leash, and strained apart,
My pack of unruly hounds! I cannot start
Them again on a quarry of knowledge they hate to hunt,
(from *Last Lesson of the Afternoon*, D.H. Lawrence)

### Hyperbole
A deliberate exaggeration used to emphasise a feeling or produce a humorous effect.
Example: I could eat a horse.

ISBN 9780170233293

I know | I need to check | I have no idea

○ ○ ○ **Imperative**
A phrase used to express a request, order or command.
Example: Go to bed now.

○ ○ ○ **Metaphor**
A form of comparison (see Simile). Instead of using 'like' or 'as', a metaphor says the two things are the same.
Example: My brother John is a pig. (This suggests that John has unpleasant manners, not that he literally is a pig.)

○ ○ ○ **Pun**
An expression that plays on different meanings of the same word or phrase. It may draw attention to an idea or create a humorous effect.
Example: Mercutio, mortally wounded, says: 'Ask for me tomorrow and you shall find me a grave man.'

○ ○ ○ **Rhetorical question**
A question that is designed to make a vivid suggestion rather than demand an answer. The writer or speaker is inviting the agreement of the audience.

○ ○ ○ **Simile**
A phrase that compares two things, using 'like' or 'as'. A simile works by suggesting the two things have characteristics that are similar. Similes add colour and vitality to writing.
Example: My brother John eats like a pig. (This suggests that John has unpleasant table manners.)

## Other

○ ○ ○ **Accent**
Intonation and pronunciation of words characteristic of a group.

○ ○ ○ **Colloquial**
An adjective used to describe everyday, spoken language which is generally informal. It is usually regarded as inappropriate in formal writing.
Example: 'Let's have a go at Hymn 96' would be inappropriate for use in a church service as it is colloquial.

I know | I need to check | I have no idea

○ ○ ○ **Connotation**
The implied or suggested meaning of a word.

○ ○ ○ **Denotation**
The dictionary meaning of a word.

○ ○ ○ **Dialect**
The given name to a language as it is spoken in a particular region of a country, having its local peculiarities of vocabulary, pronunciation, and turn of phrase.

○ ○ ○ **Dialogue**
Conversation as opposed to monologue (one speaker), narrative, descriptive writing, etc. 'Duologue' means 'restricted to two persons' and 'polylogue' means multi-participant conversation.

○ ○ ○ **Jargon**
Specialised language used by people who work together or share a common interest. The advantage of using jargon is that it helps people communicate quickly and effectively with each other as they do not have to use long-winded explanations and definitions.
Examples: hard drive, RAM, hyperlink (computer language).

○ ○ ○ **Slang**
Words or expressions that belong to a particular group of people. In most cases slang is unacceptable as appropriate language. You should only use slang in your English work if it is appropriate to both the character and the situation.
Example: It was awesome, ace, massive! (teenage slang).

## Parts of speech

○ ○ ○ **Adjective**
A describing word. It adds meaning to a noun by giving more information. A comparative adjective provides a comparison between two things and a superlative adjective between three or more.
Example: *big* dog ... *bigger* dog ... *biggest* dog.

I know | I need to check | I have no idea

○ ○ ○ **Adverb**
A word that tells us how, when or where an action takes place. Its job is to give extra meaning to verbs.
Example: Tomorrow I will build a snowman outside, *carefully*.

○ ○ ○ **Antonym**
A word that is opposite in meaning to another word.
Example: deep – shallow.

○ ○ ○ **Conjunction**
A word that joins words or sentences. Conjunctions help give variety to your writing by allowing you to have sentences of different length.
Example: The girl met the boy *and* they went for a walk on the beach.

○ ○ ○ **Noun**
A naming word. It refers to a thing, person, animal, substance, quality or place.

○ ○ ○ **Prefix**
One or more letters added to the beginning of a word to alter its meaning or form a new word.
Example: appear – *dis*appear.

○ ○ ○ **Preposition**
A word that tells us the position or place of something in relation to something else.
Example: The cat sat *on* the mat.

○ ○ ○ **Pronoun**
A word that may be used instead of a noun. Writers use pronouns to save repeating a person's name too often in a sentence or passage. Some pronouns are used to make the reader feel involved in the passage, as though the writer is talking directly to him or her.
Example: *You* know how *it* feels to quarrel with *your* best friend.

○ ○ ○ **Suffix**
One or more letters added to the end of a word to alter its meaning.
Example: grace – grace*ful*, nation – nation*al*.



ISBN 9780170233293

I know I need to check I have no idea

## Synonym
A word identical or very similar in meaning to another word. It is important to look at synonyms as they help to improve your writing and vocabulary by adding variety.
Example: hot – spicy

## Verb
A doing or being word.
Example: (1) I *walked* to school today. (2) I *was* happy.

# Poetic devices

## Alliteration
The repetition of consonant sounds, usually at the start of the word. Writers use alliteration for several reasons: it helps draw our attention to a line in a poem or passage, or a particular image, and it can slow down our reading or speed up the words in order to create an atmosphere. The last reason, usually employed by advertisers, is that it can make things easy to remember.
Example: 'A black-backed gull bent like an iron bar' has to be read slowly in order to pronounce the bs. Therefore it emphasises the strength of the wind against which the bird is flying.

## Anacoluthon
A change in grammatical structure, as in the following example: 'Is he still waiting … of course, you told me yesterday.'

## Assonance
The deliberate repetition of the same vowel sound followed by a different consonant sound. Assonance may create a musical effect, or be used to highlight imagery.
Example: 'He climbed high, singing wildly,
Clinging to the rock face
Alive, at last.'

## Blank verse
Verse with a set rhythm but no set rhyme scheme.

## Caesura
A natural pause or a break within a line of poetry, usually indicated by a punctuation mark.

I know I need to check I have no idea

## Cliché
An expression that has lost its originality and humour through constant use. The English language is full of clichés, often expressed as metaphors or similes.

## Emotive language
Language that attempts to play on people's emotions.
Example: The shopping centre was littered with decaying food scraps, empty torn plastic packets, broken glass, dumped supermarket trolleys and sad, defeated people. (The language chosen here is to make the shopping centre seem depressing.)

## End-stopped line
The lines of a stanza that have a grammatical pause at the end of each line. This technique completes an idea visually and grammatically.

## Enjambment
When the meaning of a line of poetry is completed on the next line. This technique can emphasise an idea or add to the rhythm of and flow of the lines.

## Eye rhymes
Words which are spelled alike and in most instances were once pronounced alike, but now have a different pronunciation: prove-love, daughter-laughter.

## Iambic pentameter
The metre used by Shakespeare in blank verse or in sonnets. It consists of 5 iambic feet.

## Imagery
The creation of images or pictures to help writers achieve their intended purpose.

## Metre
Is the generally regular repetition of a given pattern of accented and unaccented syllables; the metrical unit is the foot. See also rhythm.

## Onomatopoeia
When the sound of the word imitates or suggests the meaning or noise of the action described.
Example: The *buzz* of the chainsaw.

I know I need to check I have no idea

## Personification
When a non-living thing is given living characteristics or when a non-human thing is given human characteristics.
Example: The vine is strangling that tree. (This gives the idea of vine as aggressor with intent to harm and the tree as the victim.)

## Repetition
Where words and/or phrases are repeated for emphasis or special effect.
Example: It was cold that night, very, very cold.

## Rhyme
The repetition of similar sounds. It is often used in order to be pleasing to the ear and to give a piece of writing rhythm and flow. Rhyme is also used to hold certain lines of poetry together in order to link ideas and images.
Example: She left the web, she left the loom, (from *The Lady of Shallot*, Alfred Lord Tennyson).

## Rhythm
The pace or tempo at which a passage moves. Rhythm reflects the underlying emotion or meaning of a passage. It is created by the emphasis or stress placed on syllables, or words, or groups of words. It can be referred to as 'metre'. In the example below the beat/sound of the train is imitated.
Example: This is the night mail crossing the border
Bringing the cheque and the postal order (from *The Night Mail*, W.H. Auden).

## Point of view
The angle from which a piece is written. A passage may be written from its author's point of view or a narrator's point of view or an institution's point of view.

## Purpose
The reason why a passage has been written.
Examples: to inform, to amuse, to persuade or to promote a particular action.

ISBN 9780170233293

I know | I need to check | I have no idea

○○○ **Setting**
Time, place, social background.

○○○ **Sibilance**
The repetition of the consonant 's' and 'z' to give a hissing sound. The effect of sibilance is to slow the reader as 's' and 'z' take longer to say. This, in turn, emphasises the idea and can also create an onomatopoeic effect. Example: suggesting snake-like movement and sound – 'slippery, slithering, sliding snake'.

○○○ **Style**
The way a piece has been written.

○○○ **Symbolism**
A word or phrase signifying a sign or mark representing something else. A symbol brings a significant idea and all its connotations through use of a single word. Example: The dove (of peace), the cross (of Christianity)

○○○ **Target audience**
The section of the viewing public that a piece is largely aimed at or pitched to. It may be an age group, gender or ethnic group.
Example: Hairy Maclary books are targeted at preschool children.

○○○ **Theme**
The main ideas that the author/director wants us to think about.

○○○ **Tone**
The writer's attitude about the topic of the piece. It may be angry, sarcastic, passionate or sad, and so on.

## Visual

○○○ **Audience**
The designer of an image always takes into account the intended audience in order to use techniques that are likely to attract that particular group. They may be female or male, teenagers or older, ethnic groups or movie-goers.

I know | I need to check | I have no idea

○○○ **Balance**
Images aim to present a balanced effect – achieved by thinking of the space in thirds, quarters, or halves, each section needing similar proportions or elements.

○○○ **Bold lines**
Some features may be outlined to give them definition. Framing the image may also help keep the viewer's eye focused.

○○○ **Border**
Used to create an edge to an image. It focuses the viewer's eye on the page. A border can reflect the image's content, for example koru shapes on a poster for a Māori film.

○○○ **Colour**
Designers carefully select which colours they use on a static image. Designers also need to consider whether there are colours that will help represent their idea. For example, yellow usually represents warmth or happiness whereas black can represent sophistication or death.

○○○ **Contrast**
One method of gaining people's attention is by using two colours for eye-catching contrasts. Contrast can also be achieved by juxtaposing a picture with an area of text.

○○○ **Dominant visual feature**
The feature that first grabs a viewer's attention. Designers think carefully about what it is they first want people to see as it often affects whether they will look at the image more closely. It may be a picture, words or part of an illustration.

○○○ **Emotive language**
Words that are aimed at stirring emotion. Anger? Distress? Joy?

○○○ **Empty space**
There are times when empty space becomes an important technique. Empty space around the words and pictures helps to draw attention to them.

I know | I need to check | I have no idea

○○○ **Euphemism**
Saying something unpleasant in a pleasant way. Euphemisms often use positive connotations instead of negative. i.e. slender instead of scrawny, cuddly instead of fat.
Example: 'A deodorant for moist underarm areas.'

○○○ **Hyperbole**
Exaggeration for effect, usually to grab your attention.
Example: Russell Hobbs – 'generations ahead'.

○○○ **Impact**
An image needs to stand out amongst a crowd of other images. The image may be shocking, dramatic, unusual, funny or controversial.

○○○ **Imperative/command**
The use of a command to provoke actions. Advertisements are written to persuade us to act so it is not surprising the imperative is used frequently. We are asked to 'try', 'use', 'look', 'hurry on down', etc. These add force to the suggestions being made and are also designed to make it seem urgent that we buy the product.

○○○ **Layout**
How the words and pictures of an image have been put together. Everything is placed in order to create a unity of ideas and let the viewer's eye move naturally from the most important feature to the least.

○○○ **Lettering**
There are many options available with lettering: different fonts, sizes, upper or lower case, italic or bold. If an image needs to be seen from a distance then it needs to have large lettering; if the image is going to be held in a hand, such as an advertisement or flyer, there is more choice.

○○○ **Message**
The ideas contained in the image. The basic aim of an image may be to influence us to act a certain way or make a particular decision. It may be to sponsor a World Vision child, buy one product over another or attend a particular tertiary institute.


ISBN 9780170233293

I know | I need to check | I have no idea

### Neologisms
The language of advertising has contributed a generous share of new words into the English language. While purists might frown, these words sometimes achieve quite extensive use. We are invited to 'unzip' a banana or sip a drink that is 'orangemostest', or taste the 'Schweppervesence'. Neologisms help make a product appear original and retain the consumers' attention as they read the advertisement. They may also be referred to as coinage.
Many of the emotive adjectives first found their way into the world through advertising. For example: bubbly, minty, tangy, chewy, nutty, silky and spicy.

### Perspective
Images can be two dimensional (look flat) or three dimensional (have depth). You can suggest perspective on a 2D image or build depth by embossing or shadowing.

### Pictures/illustrations
It is important that a picture or visual be clear and that it is a suitable size. The chosen picture also needs to be appropriate to the image – it would be silly to use a picture of a baby to advertise a retirement village!

### Proportion
The graphic elements in an image should be in correct ratio to each other. For example, a person's head should match the size of his or her body. Proportion may be distorted for comic or dramatic effect.

### Reverse print
White text on a black background (reversing the usual black text on white). Reverse print is used to make the lettering stand out.

### Slogan
A catchphrase often linked to a company or product. For example, Nike – 'Just do it!' or The Warehouse – 'Where everyone gets a bargain'.

### Symbol
This is a word or set of words that signifies an object or event which itself signifies something else.
Example: The cross symbolises the Christian religion
The colour white represents purity and innocence.

### Tone
The mood of the writing. Personal? Colloquial? Formal? Slang?

### Unusual images
An unusual picture or layout may make people stop and look more carefully at an image. Designers are always trying to come up with new and interesting ways to catch the audience's attention.

### Use of statistics
Factual information often helps to sway a person's opinion.

### Well-known/popular faces
People like to buy something that others endorse, particularly if they know something about the product or topic. For example, Hamish Carter would be a good person to use to sell running shoes as he has a reputation as a runner.

## Film

### Close-up (CU)
Contains no background but focuses on the whole of an object or a person's head and shoulders. They may reveal human emotions or private information.

### Cut
A change from one shot to the next without using an effect such as a dissolve, wipe or fade.

### Dissolve
Occurs when one frame is gradually replaced by another so that at the mid-point of the dissolve both are visible on the screen. They can be used to show a change of location or time, but they are also used to indicate a flashback or a dream, or to show what a character is thinking.

### Editing
The post-production process where the film stock is assembled to achieve the final product. Shots and scenes are selected, arranged and ordered in the most dramatic way.

### Establishing shot (extreme long shot – ELS)
Contains a lot of landscape and gives important information about the setting, atmosphere or context in which following events will take place. It is often used at the beginning of a scene or sequence.

### Extreme close-up (ECU)
Focuses on an aspect of an object in great detail or a part of a person's face, headline of a newspaper or detail of symbols such as a police identification.

### Fade
Where the screen is black at the beginning, then gradually the image appears. A fade-out is the opposite of this. A fade can be used to suggest a passage of time, or a new location. It also suggests a special relationship between the two scenes that would not be conveyed by a simple cut.

### Full shot (FS)
Contains the whole height of any figure in the frame.

### High-angle shot
Taken when the camera is above or looking down at the figure. The main purpose of this shot is to make the object or person look small, insignificant or helpless.

ISBN 9780170233293

I know / I need to check / I have no idea

○ ○ ○ **Long shot (LS)**
Contains a fair amount of landscape or background though figures in the scene are recognisable as being human and male or female.

○ ○ ○ **Low-angle shot**
Taken when the camera is below or looking up at a figure. The main purpose of this shot is to make the object or person look large, powerful and dominant.

○ ○ ○ **Medium shot (mid shot – MS)**
Where the person is seen from the waist up. If there are two people in the shot it is called a two-shot, if there are three, a three-shot.

○ ○ ○ **Over-the-shoulder shot**
Where a shot is filmed over a character's shoulder from behind. It is usual for this shot to look towards another character and will generally be followed by a reverse-angle shot showing the face of the person whose back was to the camera. It is mostly used during conversations or interviews.

○ ○ ○ **Overhead shot**
Taken when the camera is directly above the figure.

○ ○ ○ **Pan**
When a camera moves horizontally (side to side) on its tripod. It is often used to show the vastness of a location.

○ ○ ○ **Point-of-view (POV) shot**
Where the camera becomes the eyes of one of the characters and sees things from that character's point of view.

○ ○ ○ **Tilt**
Where the camera moves upwards or downwards on its tripod to follow moving objects or reveal a scene or object which is too big to fit in one frame.

I know / I need to check / I have no idea

○ ○ ○ **Tracking**
The camera (mounted on tracks, vehicle, dolly or hand-held) follows the subject. You will frequently see this shot used during a 'chase' scene as it makes the camera appear to be following or 'tracking' the object: it makes the audience feel like they are alongside the action.

○ ○ ○ **Under shot**
Taken when the camera is directly underneath the figure. This suggests extreme power or danger.

○ ○ ○ **Wipe**
Occurs when one shot is covered up or replaced by another shot moving horizontally across the screen. A wipe is used as a transition from one scene to another and suggests a close relationship between the images.

## Oral

○ ○ ○ **Allusion/reference**
Covert, implied, indirect reference (to something or someone). For example: 'fourscore and seven years ago' alludes to the Bible in its language; 'founding forefathers' alludes to USA history

○ ○ ○ **Anecdotes**
Short stories used to help illustrate a point.

○ ○ ○ **Antithesis**
The contrast between words or ideas. Used to emphasise a difference and/or to give the effect of balance.
For example: 'He knew everything about literature except how to enjoy it.' (*Catch 22* by Joseph Heller)

I know / I need to check / I have no idea

○ ○ ○ **Audience appeal**
A good speaker knows his/her audience before he/she begins and reads his/her audience as he/she speaks. A student wanting to be voted onto his/her school's Board of Trustees will talk about current issues facing students at that school. An aspiring politican wanting to be voted in by a community facing a major issue (eg., West Coast: logging, Waihi: mining) will talk about that issue above all else.

○ ○ ○ **Body language**
How a speaker stands and moves. The use of body language adds interest to a speech.

○ ○ ○ **Emotive words**
Add impact to a speech.

○ ○ ○ **Examples/statistics**
These are best used to support an argument. If they are 'shocking' they can help capture an audience's attention and keep them listening.

○ ○ ○ **Eye-contact**
Establishes a rapport and makes an audience feel involved.

○ ○ ○ **Gesture**
They can add interest and help emphasise a point. Think of speech-making as having an animated conversation with a friend.

○ ○ ○ **Humour**
A great ice-breaker and an effective tool for keeping an audience listening if linked to either the topic, audience or the occasion.

○ ○ ○ **Intonation**
This is the way the voice rises and falls while speaking and adds atmosphere and mood.

○ ○ ○ **Listing**
Including many examples in a list form may add weight to your argument.



ISBN 9780170233293

I know / I need to check / I have no idea

### Parallelism

Comparison or correspondence of two successive passages:
'On the 4th of July we count our blessings, and there are so many to count. We're thankful for the families we love. We're thankful for the opportunities in America. We're thankful for our freedom ...'
(George W. Bush, 4 July 2002.)

### Pause

Useful for emphasising important points. It can also create suspense or be used for dramatic effect as well as offering an easy place to maintain eye-contact.

I know / I need to check / I have no idea

### Personal pronouns

These make a speech more personal and help the audience feel involved.

### Quotations

Sayings that sum up in a nutshell what a speaker wishes to convey are useful devices. Proverbs are particularly useful in this way.
For example: 'The hand that rocks the cradle rules the world.' 'Where there's a will there's a way.'
A well-known phrase is also often a cliché – repeated too often to have much effect. A quotation can give a speech an air of greater authority.

I know / I need to check / I have no idea

### Tricolon

The division of an idea into three harmonious parts, usually of increasing power.
For example:
'... government of the people, by the people, for the people' (Abraham Lincoln, President of the USA, in the Gettysburg Address at the dedication of a graveyard at Gettysburg, one of the battlefields of the American Civil War in 1863.)
'Today, our fellow citizens, our way of life, our very freedom came under attack ...'
(George Bush, President of the USA, in his address to the nation after the terrorist attack on New York, 11 September 2001.)

## Use this space to list any additional language techniques introduced to you by your teacher.

ISBN 9780170233293

# 13 Revision

## It's time to revise – ready, set, go!

External assessment for English is likely to be one of the first assessments you sit. A lot of students sit this assessment and the markers need time to get all the papers marked!

You will be offered the following external standards:

**AS 3.1** Respond critically to specified aspect(s) of studied written text(s), supported by evidence

**AS 3.2** Respond critically to specified aspect(s) of studied visual or oral text(s), supported by evidence

**AS 3.3** Respond critically to significant aspects of unfamiliar written text(s) through close reading, supported by evidence

We have assumed that you will be preparing for each Standard. We have met students who say: '*Well, I'll just prepare for the two I think I can do best in.*' This is NOT a good idea. Seriously. What if that particular Standard asks questions that really don't work for your text/s? What if you don't really understand a question? What if you panic and go blank about a text? Our best advice is to **prepare for all the Standards** offered.

## Know thyself

You have already experienced revising for external assessment, so you will know what **your personal strengths and weaknesses** are.

Aim to build on your strengths:

- I study best in the mornings.
- I need to eat first then study.
- It's best if I go to the library; so I go.

Aim to minimise your weaknesses:

- I have to turn my phone off.
- I have to promise myself chocolate AFTER I study.
- I have to get Mum to take my sisters to the park for an hour.

Yes, it's true that every student approaches revision in their own way, but there are some things that we think are just as important in Year 13 as they were previously.



ISBN 9780170233293

## A place to study

It is important that you set yourself up a study station. You will need a desk or a table, a comfortable (not too comfortable) chair, good lighting … and quiet. Make sure you have a good stock of refill, pens, pencils and highlighters, too.

If you are not able to work in your bedroom, then using a corner of the dining room table is fine. Turn off the TV. Turn off the radio. Ask Dad to take care of your little brother. You need time and space to think!

## A time to study

You probably have lots of things in your life other than school. This is the time of year when you evaluate which of these things are unavoidable and which commitments could be put on hold (or at least reduced) during the lead up to the examinations. Can you work fewer hours? Do you need to attend every team training session? Can you avoid a trip to Aunt Karen's this week?

Set up a personal weekly planner. This is likely to change each week, so create one week at a time and fill in the study you plan to do each week. Your study time may vary depending on what hours you work, your sports or family commitments. Plus, if you are having extra tutoring you can count this towards that subject for the week. You need to ensure though that if you take extra time off, you make it up somewhere else.

We are quite aware that you will have more than just English to study for. You need to work out how many subjects you have to study and the actual commitment each subject will take. The examples we have used assume you have five subjects that will have up to three external assessments each.

We have started this timetable at 9 am but if you are a 'morning person' you might prefer to do an hour's study between 6.30 and 7.30 am!

### Timetable 1: For during the school week

| | Mon | Tues | Wed | Thurs | Fri | Sat | Sun |
|---|---|---|---|---|---|---|---|
| 9.00-10.00 | | | | | | | Biology |
| 10.00-11.00 | | | | | | | |
| 11.00-12.00 | | | | | | | English |
| 12.00-1.00 | | | | | | | |
| 1.00-2.00 | | | | | | | Stats |
| 2.00-3.00 | | | | | | | |
| 3.00-4.00 | | | | | | English | Geography |
| 4.00-5.00 | Geography | Classical Studies | Stats | Classical Studies | | English | |
| 5.00-6.00 | | | | | | | Classical Studies |
| 6.00-7.00 | English | Stats | Biology | Geography | | | |
| 7.00-8.00 | | | | | | | Biology |
| 8.00-9.00 | | | | | | | |

ISBN 9780170212953

When school finishes you should change your timetable to reflect the increase in the time available for study. Take a look at the example below:

**Timetable 2: For when school has finished**

| | Mon | Tues | Wed | Thurs | Fri | Sat | Sun |
|---|---|---|---|---|---|---|---|
| 9.00-10.00 | English | Biology | | Classical Studies | English | | |
| 10.05-11.05 | | Classical Studies | Stats | Geography | Biology | | Stats |
| | | | | | | | English |
| 11.30-12.30 | Stats | English | Geography | English | Stats | | Classical Studies |
| 12.35-1.05 | English | | | Stats | | | Biology |
| | | | | | | | |
| 2.00-3.00 | Biology | Stats | Classical Studies | | Geography | Classical Studies | English |
| 3.05-4.00 | Classical Studies | Geography | Biology | Biology | Classical Studies | English | |
| | | | | | | | Classical Studies |
| 4.30-5.30 | Geography | | English | Biology | | Geography | Stats |
| | | | | | | | |
| 7.00-8.00 | Geography | English | Biology | Stats | | | |

*You will find blank copies of these grids for you to create your own timetable at www.cengage.co.nz/ach-eng-y13*

You will notice that there is enough space to add a sixth subject if you need to, or to add extra hours to subjects that you find more difficult. Of course you can vary your timetable to suit your life's pattern.

You need to make sure that when you are not studying that you are doing something other than sitting and watching TV! Getting some fresh air is a great way to recharge your batteries. It could be a swim, a walk (even if only to the letterbox!), a game of basketball etc.

Eat good, healthy food and drink plenty of water. Sleep is also a vital part of a good study programme – burning the midnight oil is not a useful technique for most of us.

## What to study

In the past *Achievement English* books have given students a detailed revision programme, however as a Year 13 student it really is time for you to do this for yourself.

We are sure that your teacher will give you some ideas for a study programme. Here is a check list of things we think you should be doing in the final weeks of preparation before your Level 3 external assessments.



ISBN 9780170212953

## PHASE ONE: Get organised

- Sort EVERYTHING! All your materials from English classes, revision lessons, personal study, tutoring etc into a divided ring binder or separate folders.
- Check your computer files. Sort, rename, place in folders etc. Print anything worth annotating.
- Check your entire room, bag, books for important 'missing' pages.
- If you were absent for any time during the year make sure you have any notes you may have missed. Ask your friends, ask your teacher.
- Sort all your notes into a logical order. Re-writing scrappy notes tidily is a great way of reminding yourself about the topic.
- Ensure you have a copy of all texts you have studied this year. This may mean getting extended texts re-issued or visiting a library (or even buying your own copy!).

## PHASE TWO: The hard yards

- Re-read any books, novels, short stories, poetry, plays or other written texts you have studied during the year and rewatch the film you will be using. You will pick up additional detail once you know a text well.
- Study your notes. Highlight important points that you want to remember.
- Some people like to make cue cards to flick through as an easy reminder of key information.
- Go through the essays you have written during the year. Take note of your teacher's marking. If there is anything you don't understand, ask them to explain.
- You might like to have another go at an essay that was not so successful. We are sure your teacher will mark it for you.
- Go back through *Achievement English @ Year 13*. It is full of good advice – take it! Complete any unfinished sections.
- Throughout the year you will have been given sample NCEA Level 3 essays. Re-read. You can find more on the NZQA website.
- Form a study group – remember that a study group does not have to be a group of friends! Swap essays, notes and ideas. Discuss things you need to clarify.
- If you are writing a practice essay don't limit yourself to a minimum number of words.
- Although the examiner doesn't want to read a rote-learnt essay, learning your quotations off by heart is an excellent thing to do.

## PHASE THREE: The night before

Relax ... you have done the hard yards. The best thing you can do for yourself at this point is get a good night's sleep. Burning the midnight oil won't help your brain function in the morning.

ISBN 9780170212953

## An aside on ... what to study

### Studying for assessment of your texts

1 Know the text well.
2 Spell its title and author/director's name correctly.
3 Learn a few short quotations that might be used for examples in several essay questions.
4 Know the principal characters' names exactly.
5 List the major theme/themes for revision.
6 Learn details of the setting (time, place, social background).
7 Practise writing to time (you will probably do this in class).

### Studying for assessment of unfamiliar texts

The studies on texts that you have completed through the year will have given you the experience of understanding and responding to texts with guidance. In this assessment you have to use those skills without the benefit of a teacher's voice, your fellow classmates' ideas, or a lot of time. It's a great opportunity to show that you CAN read, understand and analyse text all by yourself. Yes, you can.

1 You will have completed several close reading exercises in class (and through *Achievement English @ Year 13*). Revisiting these texts and the questions you were asked and your answers would be useful.
2 Answer the questions again, improving on your first attempt.
3 Make sure you have the process off by heart:
   - read the text
   - read the questions
   - read the text again
   - annotate the text (on the page in the assessment, in class if allowed)
   - think
   - plan
   - write.

   For some students, this seems like a very long process in an assessment where you just want to get on with answering the question. However, if you follow this process (briskly) you will find that it saves time in the end, because you will know what you want to say when you start to write. It usually means better results, too! Try it out in a class assessment before the real thing.

### Using the Internet for study

You will have studied longer texts, like novels and plays, in class. When it comes to writing about these texts it is very tempting to go to the Internet and copy what is written there. It can be very useful to read what others have written, especially if those others are knowledgeable. In fact, if you pick your information wisely you can supplement your class notes and find some new material to refresh your memory about your text. Your teacher may well have recommended useful works of criticism to help you make complete responses about the text you are studying.

However, as you know, there is no quality control on the Internet so what we suggest is:

- Plan your own response to the text first
- Then do some reading of criticism written by others
- Then go back to what you have written and see if you might add to or rework your own ideas.

It's what you think that counts!


ISBN 9780170212953